ELVIS
THE EARLY YEARS
A 2001 FACT ODYSSEY

By Jim Curtin

with Renata Ginter

Celebrity Books • Nashville, Tennessee

Published by
Celebrity Books
a division of Hambleton-Hill Publishing, Inc.
1501 County Hospital Road
Nashville, TN 37218

For a free catalogue of titles
or to order more copies of this book,
please call (800) 327-5113

ISBN: 1-58029-106-6

Library of Congress Cataloging-In-Publication Data:
Curtin, Jim.
Elvis, the early years : a 2001 fact odyssey / by Jim Curtin, with Renata Ginter.
p.   cm.
ISBN 1-58029-106-6 (pbk.)
1. Presley, Elvis, 1935-1977 Childhood and youth.   2. Presley, Elvis, 1935-1977
Miscellanea. 3. Country musicians--United States Biography.   I. Ginter, Renata.
II. Title. III. Title: 2001 fact odyssey. IV. Title: Two thousand and one fact odyssey.
ML420.P96C92   1999
782.42166'092--dc21   99-33781
[B]   CIP

Cover design: John Laughlin
All photos from the collection of James J. Curtin Archives,
The Elvis Empire™

First printing, August 1999
Printed in the USA

10 9 8 7 6 5 4 3 2 1

 Dedications

In memory of my beloved parents,
James J. Curtin, Jr. and Louise M. Curtin

In memory of my grandparents,
James J. Curtin, Sr. and Eileen Kennedy Curtin
&
Camillo Faione and Catherine Faione

In memory of my great-grandmother,
Mary Vespi

Also dedicated to the memory of Renata's grandparents,
Jozef and Maria Zawazdki

And to the Ginter family,
Krzysztof, Leokadia, Kasia, Robert, and Gregory

A special dedication to the Presley and Smith Families—
May God Bless Them All!

James J. Curtin

Acknowledgements

Special thanks to Sandra Laughlin and Van Hill,
two wonderful people!
Thanks a million for all your help, friendship, and great business.

Also to all the hard-working people at Celebrity Books, especially:
John Laughlin, Art Director
You made my books look great! Thank you!
Bethany Snyder, Editor
Thank you for all your great editing!

My sincerest thanks to my writer and assistant, Renata.
You've helped my dreams come true!
Thank you from the bottom of my heart!

—Jim

My heartfelt thanks to Jim Curtin.
You allowed me into your life and archives, and gave me the
opportunity to become an important part of
your wonderful series of books on Elvis Presley. Thank you!

—Renata

Also special thanks and acknowledgments to:
The Graceland Estate
Elvis Presley Enterprises

Photo Credits: Vester Presley, the Presley Family, EPE, Graceland, Billy Smith, Milam Junior High School, L.C. Humes High School, Mildred Scrivener, *Memphis Press Scimitar*, Crown Electric, Sam Phillips/Sun Studios, WREC Radio/Marion Keisker, Bob Neal, Ed Sullivan/CBS, Jordanaires, Steve Allen/NBC, Milton Berle, Dorsey's *Stage Show*/CBS, Wink Martindale, March of Dimes, WorldWide Photo, UPI, Twentieth Century Fox, Alfred Wertheimer, WHBQ/Dewey Phillips, Popular Tunes Record Store, RCA, MGM Studios, The River Group (The Elvis Collection)

And special thanks to the Presley-Pressley Onelist (www.onelist.com) for their help with the Presley-Pressley family tree.

Introduction

This book was written with two purposes. The first was to "educate" Elvis fans by providing little known facts about the life of Elvis Presley; the second was to give people something to read about Elvis that is completely different from the hundreds of Elvis books already published. You will find that this is a different kind of book, a book you can enjoy, relax with, and pick up without losing your place.

Many of you may ask yourselves, "Why such a title as *Elvis, the Early Years: A 2001 Fact Odyssey*?" There are two reasons for this as well. First, because the classical song *Also Sprach Zarathustra* from the movie *2001: A Space Odyssey* was used to dramatize Elvis's entrances during his concerts in the 1970's. It is as widely associated with Elvis as his trademark sideburns and flashy jumpsuits; it is also a title that Elvis fans will remember! Second, the number 2001 relates to the number of facts included in this first volume.

You might also ask yourself, "How do I know that these facts are true and accurate?" Thousands of hours of research were put into the making of this book, and each fact has been researched repeatedly to ensure that dates, places, and names are accurate. You will not find another compilation of Elvis facts that is more accurate, in-depth, or interesting than this book.

This first volume chronicles Elvis's early years, as the title suggests, and covers such topics as the history of Tupelo, Mississippi, and Memphis, Tennessee, Elvis's ancestry, his family, his early childhood, his school years, his rise to fame, and everything else you would want to know about the early King of Rock-n-Roll! Each fact is numbered and is in chronological order.

Everything and anything you ever wanted to know about Elvis Aron Presley will be included in subsequent volumes of this series, including information about his movies, his Army career, his concerts, the 1960's, and beyond.

So please, kick your shoes off, put on your favorite Elvis record or CD, ease yourself into your favorite seat, and relax as you read this treasure trove of 2001 facts!

Jim Curtin

Elvis's Paternal Family Tree

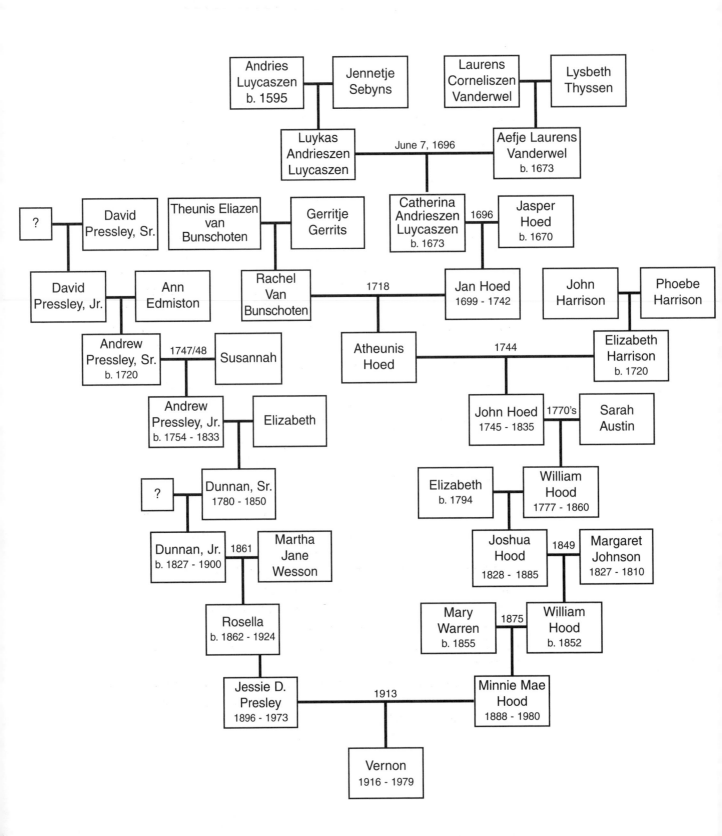

Elvis's Maternal Family Tree

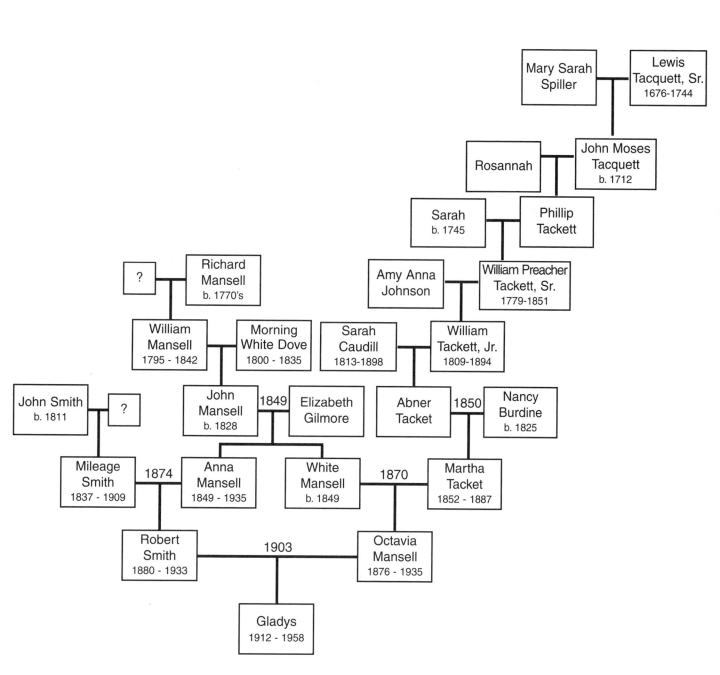

Rosella Presley, Elvis's paternal great-grandmother.

The Early Years

1   Two of the earliest known paternal ancestors of Elvis Presley were Andries Luycaszen, born in 1595 in Frederickstad, Denmark, and his wife, Jennetje (Sebyns) Luycaszen. They were Elvis's grandparents eleven generations removed.

2   In the very early part of the 1600's, Laurens Corneliszen van der Wel married Lysbeth Thyssen. These ancestors of Elvis are on the same level of his family tree as the Luycaszens.

3   Jasper Hoed was born in 1670. He is the earliest Hoed (Hood) to be traced to Elvis's paternal family tree. Jasper was Minnie Mae (Hood) Presley's grandfather seven generations removed.

4   Andries and Jennetje's son, Luykas Andrieszen, married Aefje Laurens, the daughter of Laurens and Lysbeth van der Wel. Their daughter, Cathrina Andries, was born in New Amsterdam, New York, in 1673.

5   On June 7, 1696, Catherina Andries van der Wel married Jasper Hoed and moved to Kingston, New York. They had four children: Jan, Aefje, Luykas, and Thomas.

6   Jan Hoed, who was born in 1699, married Rachel van Bunschoten in 1718 in an old Dutch Reform Church in Kingston, New York. They had six children: Antheunis, Johannes, Jacobus, Cathrina, Gerritjen, and Rebekka.

7   Rachel van Bunschoten's parents were Theunis Eliazen van Bunschoten and Gerritje Gerrits.

8   The Mansells, Elvis's maternal ancestors, first immigrated from Ulster, Scotland, to Ireland in the 1700's.

9   The name "Pressley" is said to be linked with the Bronze Age Prescelli tribe of South Wales. The name is derived from the English root name PREOSTLEAH, which means "a dweller in the priest's meadow." In Scotland, the name had three spellings: Pressley, Preslie, and Presslie. The original Gaelic spelling of the Presley name is PREASLEY.

10   David Pressley was the earliest Pressley to be tracked down in Elvis's paternal family tree. He fathered David Pressley, Jr. who had one son, Andrew, in 1720.

11   On February 26, 1742, Jan Hoed died in Kingston, New York.

12   Antheunis Hoed married Elizabeth Harrison (b. 1720) in 1744 in Augusta, Virginia. Her parents were John and Phoebe Harrison.

13   Andrew Pressley was the first of his line to live in the United States. After immigrating from Scotland in 1745, he settled in Anson County, North Carolina. He and his wife, Susannah, were married in 1747/48.

14   Antheunis and Elizabeth Hoed moved to Frederick County, Virginia, and had nine children: John (b. 1745), Tunis, Jr., Solomon, Reuben, Elizabeth, Phoebe, Rachel, Mary, and Lydia.

15   Sometime after his marriage to Elizabeth, Antheunis Hoed changed the spelling of his last name to "Hood."

16   Andrew Pressley, Sr. had five children with Susannah: a daughter (name unknown), John (b. 1748), Andrew Jr. (b. 1754), Thomas (b. 1766), and Peter.

17   In the 1770's, Richard Mansell became the first of Elvis's maternal ancestors to be born in the United States. Richard, who was the earliest Mansell to be tracked down in Elvis's family tree, was born in the state of Tennessee. His parents had immigrated to the United States a few years prior to Richard's birth.

18   The name MANSELL means "man from LeMans" in French. During the Norman conquest, many Mansells traveled to England and Scotland, where Elvis's ancestors immigrated from in 1718.

19   In the 1770's, John Hood married Sarah (Sallie) Austin, who was born in North Carolina. They had seven sons: William (b.1777 in North Carolina), Austin, James, Amos, Isaac, Robert, and Osborn.

20   Andrew Pressley, Jr. bought land in Lancaster County, South Carolina. A blacksmith, he later moved to Hawkins County, Tennessee, where he married a woman named Elizabeth. Their son, Dunnan, was born in 1780 in North Carolina.

21   In 1781, during the American Revolution (1775-1783), Andrew Pressley, Jr. fought with the Continental Army in the battle of Eutaw Springs.

22   In 1795, Richard Mansell, Elvis's great-great-great-great-grandfather, settled in South Carolina and fathered a son named William.

23   Morning White Dove (1800-1835), a Cherokee Indian, was born in Hamilton County, Alabama. She became Elvis's great-great-great-grandmother.

24 The first Smith to be included in the Mansell family was John Smith, born in 1811. He was related to the Mansells through the marriage of his son, Mileage, to Anna Mansell.

25 William Mansell served in the army under Andrew Jackson when he was 22 years old.

26 Elvis's ancestor, William Mansell, moved to North Carolina and then to Tennessee before acquiring land and building a home in Marion County, Alabama.

27 William Mansell married Morning White Dove in 1818. They had three children: John, born in 1828; Morning Dizenie, born in 1832; and James, born in 1835. Morning White Dove died giving birth to James.

28 Morning White Dove had one sister, Mapy. Mapy married Moses Purser, William Mansell's best friend.

29 Dunnan Pressley, Sr., Elvis's great-great-great-grandfather, was a North Carolina farmer in the 1820's.

30 The first Jewish person in Gladys Presley's family tree was Nancy J. Burdine, her great-great-grandmother. Nancy was born in 1825.

31 Elvis's paternal great-great-grandfather, Dunnan Pressley, Jr., was born in Madison, Tennessee, in 1827.

32 William Hood married a woman named Elizabeth who was born in North Carolina in 1794. They had six children: Elizabeth, Hiram, Robert, Joshua (b. September 13, 1828, in Alabama), Charles Buren, and James R.

33   Andrew Pressley, Jr. applied for the Revolutionary War pension on March 17, 1833, at the age of 80. In 1779, he was drafted and served three months under Captain Randleman. It was during the Revolutionary War that Andrew got to know George Washington.

34   In 1835, John Hood died in Alabama.

35   John Smith fathered a son, Mileage Obediah Smith, in 1837. Mileage was Elvis's great-grandfather.

36   William Mansell, Gladys Smith's great-great-grandfather, died in 1842.

37   Elvis's great-great-grandfather, Dunnan Pressley, Jr., fought in the Mexican-American War in 1847 and also served as a Confederate soldier in the Civil War.

38   John Mansell married Elizabeth Gilmore in Hamilton County, Alabama, in 1849. The couple had either nine or ten children, including Anna, born October 25, 1849, and White. Gladys Smith Presley was the granddaughter of both Anna and White.

39   Dunnan Pressley, Jr., Vernon Presley's great-grandfather, was married to four different women—all at the same time!

40   On December 20, 1849, Joshua Hood married Margaret Johnson (b. 1827) in St. Clair County, Alabama. They had six children: James, William (b. April 1852 in Mississippi), Robert A., John T., Harrison, and Osburn.

41   In 1850, Abner Tackett married Nancy J. Burdine. They were one set of Elvis's great-great-grandparents. Abner's paternal family tree has been traced back four additional generations, beginning with his

Jessie D. McClowell Pressley, Elvis's paternal grandfather.

father, Lancaster Tackett, followed by Phillip Tackett, John Moses Tacquett, and Lewis Tacquett, Sr.

42 Dunnan Pressley, Sr. died in 1850.

43 In 1852, Abner and Nancy Tackett became the parents of twins named Martha and Jerome. The twins were born in Saltillo, Mississippi, and were among the earliest twins documented in Elvis's maternal family tree.

44 Andrew Pressley, Jr. died in 1856 at the age of 101.

45 During the Civil War, S.E. Toof, publisher of *The Memphis Daily Appeal*, bought a farm consisting of 500 acres in Whitehaven, Memphis. He named the farm "Graceland" after his daughter, Grace.

46 William Hood, Elvis's great-great-great-grandfather, died in 1860 in Itawamba County, Mississippi.

47 On August 15, 1861, Dunnan Pressley, Jr. married Martha Jane Wesson. They had two daughters, Rosalinda and Rosella (b. February 1862). Dunnan was Elvis's great-great-grandfather.

48 Colonel Tom Parker's father, Adam van Kuijk, was born in Raamsdonk, Holland, in 1866.

49 William Robert Hunt was born in 1867. He grew up to be the doctor who delivered Elvis Aron and Jesse Garon Presley in 1935.

50 The Peabody Hotel, located at 149 Union Avenue in Memphis, Tennessee, opened for business in 1869. Rebuilt in 1925, it later served as the location of Elvis's senior prom.

51   Rosella Wesson Pressley, Elvis's paternal great-grandmother, was never married but had nine children. Among them were Joseph, Noah, Calhoun, and Jessie.

52   On January 22, 1870, White Mansell married Martha Tackett in Saltillo, Mississippi. At the time, he was 37 years old and she was 25. White met Martha when he moved next door to her family; Martha was just 16 at the time. White and Martha were Gladys Smith's maternal grandparents.

53   On December 13, 1874, Mileage Smith married Anna Mansell. The couple had seven children: James, William, Hal, John, Tabatha, Belle, and Robert. Mileage and Anna were Gladys Smith's paternal grandparents.

54   On September 20, 1875, William Hood married Mary L. Warren (b. October 1855, in Mississippi) in Itawamba County, Mississippi. They had eight children: Manerva, Harrison, Sally, William, Minnie Mae, Ophie D., Lou A., and Alice.

55   In 1876, A. Schwab's Dry Goods Store opened at 163 Beale Street in Memphis. The store's motto was, "If you can't find it at Schwab's, you're better off without it." Elvis and his parents shopped there after moving to Memphis.

56   Octavia Lavinia Mansell, Gladys Smith's mother, was born to White and Martha Mansell in Saltillo, Mississippi, in 1876. Octavia had three siblings: Melissa, Ida, and Jehru.

57   Colonel Parker's mother, Maria Elisabeth Ponsie, was born on September 2, 1876.

58 In 1880, John Mansell left Elizabeth for her sister, Rebecca, and fathered children with her as well. Several years later, he also deserted Rebecca. White Mansell then took over the responsibility not only of caring for his wife and their four children, but also that of caring for his mother, his two sisters, and his Aunt Rebecca and her two children, who were his half-siblings.

59 O.K. Houck Piano & Music Company opened in 1883 at 121 Union Avenue in Memphis. In the 1950's, the store, owned by Jesse F. Houck and E. Frank Preston, sold pianos and sheet music. The store's telephone number was 8-0371. Elvis traded in his guitar at this store in 1956.

60 Nipper, the RCA-Victor dog, was born in Bristol, England, in 1884 and lived until 1895. Nipper's master was John Daggert.

61 On April 17, 1885, Joshua Hood died in Mississippi. He was Elvis's great-great-grandfather.

62 Martha Tackett Smith, Gladys Presley's maternal grandmother, died in 1887. After her death, her husband, White Mansell, married Sarah Cordelia "Dealy" Kemp, who had a daughter named Ann. White was 50 years old at the time of his marriage to Sarah.

63 Elvis's paternal grandmother, Minnie Mae Hood, was born on June 17, 1888, in Fulton, Mississippi, to William Hood and Mary L. Warren Hood.

64 Minnie Mae Hood's family owned a large farm and was financially well-off. Minnie Mae was Vernon Presley's mother.

65 Jennifer "Jennie" Allensworth, one of Elvis's favorite teachers at L.C. Humes High School, was born in 1889.

66 Susan Johnson, Elvis's L.C. Humes High School homeroom teacher in 1949, was born in Batesville, Mississippi, on October 7, 1889.

67 Gladys Smith's parents, Robert Lee Smith and Octavia "Doll" Mansell, were cousins. Robert's mother, Anna Mansell, and Octavia's father, White Mansell, were brother and sister.

68 Jessie D. McClowell Pressley, Elvis's paternal grandfather, was born in Tupelo, Mississippi, on April 9, 1896.

69 The William Morris Agency was founded in 1898 by William Morris. Originally organized for vaudeville acts and theaters, the agency went on to represent motion pictures, radio, record labels and artists, concerts, fairs, night clubs, and television. The agency represented Elvis from the 1950's on. Elvis's agent at William Morris, Abe Lastfogel, was born on December 15, 1900.

70 Calhoun Pressley was born on May 9, 1899, to Rosella Pressley. Calhoun was Elvis's great uncle. He was living in Missouri at the time of his death in 1984.

71 Dunnan Pressley, Jr., Vernon Presley's great-great-grandfather, died in 1900.

72 Tom Parker's parents, Maria Elisabeth Ponsie and Adam van Kuijk, were married on May 10, 1900.

73 Joseph van Kuijk was born in Breda, Holland, in September 1900. He was Tom Parker's brother.

74 RCA (Radio Corporation of America) was founded in 1901 as Victor Records.

75 Adrianna van Kuijk, Tom Parker's sister, was born in Breda, Holland, in 1902.

76 On August 2, 1903, Elvis's cousin, Mannie Doshia Pressley (b. July 22, 1886), married 60-year-old Joshua Steele at the tender age of 15. They had five children. One of Rosella Pressley's daughters, Doshia, was the last recorded widow of a Civil War veteran when Joshua died in 1914. Doshia lived to be 96 years old, passing away on January 12, 1983.

77 Robert Lee Smith married his cousin, Octavia Mansell, on September 20, 1903, at the Church of God in Union Grove, Mississippi. The service was performed by Reverend Martin. The couple eventually had nine children.

78 Robert and Octavia's was not the only marriage between cousins in Elvis's family tree. White Mansell's nephew, Gains Mansell, married Ada Mansell, who was Octavia's sister.

79 Vernon Presley's uncle, Noah Pressley (b. August 29, 1891), married Christine Roberts in the early 1900's. Their three children were named Sales, Reubel, and Gordon.

80 Marie van Kuijk was born in Breda, Holland, in 1904. She was Tom Parker's sister.

81 Naomi Stiers was born in 1904. In 1955, she became president of the very first Elvis Presley Fan Club, which was based in Houston, Texas.

82 Effie Smith was the first child of Robert Smith and Octavia "Doll" Smith. She was born in 1904 and died a year later.

The two room shack at 306 Old Saltillo Road in Tupelo, Mississippi, where Elvis was born.

83   Robert and Octavia "Doll" Smith's second child, Lillian, was born in 1906.

84   Nel van Kuijk, Tom Parker's sister, was born in Breda, Holland, in 1907.

85   In 1908, Robert and Doll Smith were blessed with another healthy daughter, Levalle. She married Edward Smith and had two sons, Carroll and Gene.

86   In 1908, Susan Johnson graduated from Sardis High School and went on to teach in Mississippi. She also taught at the Leath School in Memphis for eight years, beginning in 1914. Susan was one of Elvis's teachers at L.C. Humes High School in Memphis.

87   Hy Gardner was born in 1909. He interviewed Elvis on his show in 1956.

88   The blues was born on Beale Street in 1909 after William Christopher (W.C.) Handy wrote the song "Boss Crump Blues" for the Mayor of Memphis. The song was later renamed "Memphis Blues." It was reported that Elvis saw W.C. Handy perform on Beale Street in the early 1950's.

89   Mileage Smith, Elvis's great-grandfather, died in 1909.

90   Andreas van Kuijk, known to the world as the infamous Colonel Tom Parker, was born in Breda, Holland, on June 26, 1909.

91   Engelina van Kuijk was born in Breda, Holland, in 1910. She was Tom Parker's sister.

92   In 1910, Robert and Doll Smith had a fourth daughter, Rhetha.

93   Elvis's great-great-grandmother, Margaret Johnson, died on April 13, 1910, in Itawamba County, Mississippi.

94   Scotty Moore's parents, Winfield Scott Moore, Sr. and Mattie Hefley, were married on August 7, 1910.

95   Scotty Moore's older brother, Carney, was born on August 31, 1911.

96   Gladys Love Smith was born to Robert and Doll Smith on April 25, 1912, in Pontotoc County, Mississippi. Gladys was born with brown eyes and dark hair and was the fifth girl in a family of nine siblings. Robert's first cousin, Leila Love Smith, gave baby Gladys her family Bible after learning that Doll had given Leila's middle name to her baby.

97   Tom Parker's brother, Ad van Kuijk, was born in Breda, Holland, in 1913.

98   Minnie Mae Hood married Jessie D. McClowell Pressley on July 20, 1913, in Mississippi. She was twenty-five years old; he was just seventeen.

99   Jessie and Minnie Mae Pressley had six children: Vernon, Vester, Nashval, Delta Mae, Gladys Earline, and Lorene.

100   Minnie Mae Pressley chose the unusual name "Elvis" for her son Vernon's middle name.

101   Andreas van Kuijk (Tom Parker) went to a Catholic, all-boys school on Breda's Karrestraut in Holland in 1913.

102   After fathering five daughters, Gladys Smith's father, Robert, wondered if he was ever going to have a son. His prayers were answered on October 3, 1914, when Travis was born. Travis lived until 1973.

103 ASCAP, the American Society of Composers, Authors and Publishers, was established in 1914 by Nathan Burkan. Elvis's recordings were registered with this organization.

104 Minnie Mae Pressley, Vernon's mother, decided to change the spelling of her last name to "Presley." She taught her children to spell their last name with one 's' as well.

105 Vester Presley, Elvis's uncle, was born on September 11, 1914. His Social Security number was 428-12-0794.

106 In 1915, there was an actual Heartbreak Hotel. The two-story brick inn was located on SR 523 off of US 41 in Kenansville, Florida. Mae Axton Boren was inspired to write about it after hearing a news report of a suicide that had occurred there. She gave the song to Elvis to record in 1955.

107 Scotty Moore's brother, Edwin, was born on January 24, 1915.

108 Clarence Saunders, who lived at 1867 Vinton Avenue, opened the first Piggly Wiggly store in Memphis, Tennessee, in 1916. It was considered the first supermarket. Elvis shopped there in his later years.

109 Vernon Elvis Presley was born on April 19, 1916, in Fulton, Mississippi. He was born with blue eyes and blonde hair.

110 Vester Presley was eighteen months old when his brother, Vernon, was born.

111 James L. Ballard was born in Tupelo, Mississippi, in 1916. He served as Mayor of Tupelo for 20 years, including the time that Elvis lived there.

112 Johanna van Kuijk, Tom Parker's sister, was born in Breda, Holland, in 1916.

113 Robert Neal Hopgood was born on January 16, 1917, in the Congo. He and his family moved to the United States in 1930, where they lived in Kentucky. Known as Bob Neal, he became Elvis's first manager.

114 Tracy Smith, son of Robert and Doll Smith and brother of Gladys, was born a deaf-mute on February 20, 1917.

115 Scotty Moore's brother, Ralph, was born on May 2, 1917.

116 Marion Keisker, commonly thought of as the first person to "discover" Elvis, was born on September 23, 1917.

117 Jan van Kuijk was born in Breda, Holland, in 1918. He was Tom Parker's brother.

118 Sales and Gordon Pressley were the first set of twins recorded in Vernon Presley's family tree. They were born on July 17, 1918.

119 Clettes Smith, Gladys's sister, was born to Robert and Doll Smith on September 14, 1919. She married Vester Presley.

120 Dr. William Robert Hunt, the man who delivered Elvis Aron and Jesse Garon Presley, started his medical practice in Tupelo, Mississippi, in 1919. His office was located at 214 West Main Street, above Riley's Jewelry. It has been reported that Dr. Hunt was also Gladys's Sunday School teacher.

121 In 1919, when Andreas van Kuijk (Tom Parker) was in the fifth grade, he worked at the Great Pony Circus in Breda, Holland.

122 As a child, Tom Parker owned his own mini-circus. He charged admission to other children to see the antics of his goat, rabbit, and crow.

123 Gladys Smith spent only four months out of the year in school because she was needed to help out at home.

124 Gladys Smith enjoyed playing basketball and was quite good at it.

125 James Wagner, Priscilla (Beaulieu) Wagner's biological father, was born to Kathryn and Harold Wagner in 1920.

126 Elisha Matthew "Bitsy" Mott was born in Arcadia, Florida, in 1920. Colonel Parker's wife's brother, he went on to become friends with Elvis and toured with him in 1955 and 1956.

127 Priscilla (Beaulieu) Wagner's maternal uncle, Albert Iversen, Jr., was born to Albert and Lorraine Iversen in 1922.

128 Robert Smith, Gladys's father, was blessed with another son, Johnny, in 1922. The last of Gladys's siblings, Johnny lived until 1968 and never married.

129 Samuel Cornelius "Sam" Phillips was born in Florence, Alabama, on January 5, 1923. Raised on a farm on the Tennessee River, he became the owner of Sun Studios.

130 Coletta's Italian Restaurant, located at 1036 South Parkway, opened in Memphis in 1923. They served authentic Italian food and old world specialties. Elvis enjoyed Italian food, and often dined at Coletta's.

131 Tom Parker's sister, Marie van Kuijk, ran away to a Franciscan convent in 1923.

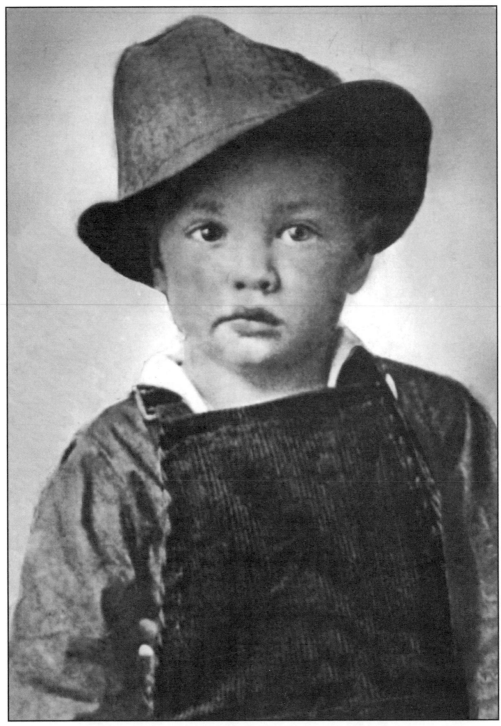

First baby photo of Elvis, taken on January 7, 1938, the day before his third birthday.
Elvis hated having his picture taken; his mother used a peanut to coax him into posing quietly.

132   Sales Pressley, Vernon Presley's cousin, married Annie Cloud sometime during the 1920's. Annie later worked at the Tupelo Garment Factory with Gladys Love Smith, where the two became good friends.

133   Rosella Pressley, Elvis's great-grandmother, died in 1924.

134   In 1924, Vernon Presley dropped out of school. He was in the third grade.

135   Priscilla (Beaulieu) Wagner's maternal uncle, James Iversen, was born to Albert and Lorraine Iversen in 1924.

136   As a teen, Gladys Smith attended dances at the Tupelo Dance Pavilion.

137   Gladys Smith's favorite dance was the "Charleston."

138   John Daniel "JD" Sumner was born on November 19, 1924.

139   As a teenager, Gladys Smith suffered from depression and nervous spells, and even had attacks of "the vapors."

140   Davada "Dee" Elliott, daughter of James Wright Elliott and Bessie Mae Heath, was born in Clarksville, Tennessee, on January 19, 1925. In 1960, she became Vernon Presley's second wife.

141   In August of 1925, Marie van Kuijk, Tom Parker's sister, officially became a Franciscan nun.

142   Adam van Kuijk, Tom Parker's father, died on July 6, 1925, at the age of 59.

143   The East Tupelo Consolidated School, where Elvis was a student,

opened in 1926. It was later renamed Lawhon Elementary School after superintendent Ross Lawhon, who was born on October 16, 1893.

144   Anne Lillian Iversen, Priscilla (Beaulieu) Wagner's mother, was born in 1926. She was of Norwegian heritage.

145   Susan Johnson, one of Elvis's teachers, began teaching at L.C. Humes High School in 1926.

146   Dewey Mills Phillips was born on May 13, 1926. He became a popular Memphis disc jockey and the first to play Elvis's debut record in 1954.

147   William Patton "Bill" Black was born on September 17, 1926. He was a member of Elvis's Blue Moon Boys band.

148   Andreas van Kuijk (Tom Parker) left his hometown of Breda, Holland, for Rotterdam and then returned briefly in 1927 at the age of 18. Family problems were the cause of his flight to the United States two years later.

149   George Constantine Nichopoulos was born in Ridgway, Pennsylvania, in 1927. Known as "Dr. Nick," he was Elvis's doctor in the 1970's.

150   Scotty Moore's sister, Mildred Lee, was born on August 14, 1913. She died from pneumonia on May 16, 1928, at the age of 14.

151   Francis Barroud painted a life-like painting of Nipper the dog which was used on RCA's "His Master's Voice" label in 1929. Before that, it was used by the Gramophone Company and then the Victor Talking Machine Company.

152 Andreas van Kuijk illegally immigrated to the United States in 1929. He settled in Huntington, West Virginia, and changed his name to Thomas A. Parker. His social security number was 267-01-1426. He joined the US Army and was stationed in Fort Barrabas, Florida. He was later transferred to the Schoffield Barracks in Hawaii.

153 Steve Sholes joined RCA-Victor in 1929. He had just graduated school, and worked as a messenger in the radio department. He was the person who signed Elvis to RCA-Victor.

154 Elvis's cousin, Carroll Jay "Junior" Smith, was born to Edward and Levalle Smith in 1930.

155 Anna Mansell Smith, Gladys's paternal grandmother, died at the age of 81 and was buried in the family plot at Unity Cemetery.

156 During Vernon Presley's adolescence and teenage years, he was a sleepwalker.

157 Elvis's cousin, Harold Loyd, was born to Rhetha Smith Loyd in 1931.

158 Adrianna van Kuijk's first husband's name was Toon van Garp. Adrianna was Tom Parker's sister.

159 Edmund Keahola Parker, son of Arthur and Eva Parker, was born in Honolulu, Hawaii, on March 19, 1931. Ed became the "Father of American Karate," as well as Elvis's Kempo instructor and good friend.

160 George Nichopoulos and his family moved from Ridgway, Pennsylvania to Anniston, Alabama, in the early 1930's. George served as Elvis's doctor in the 1970's.

Elvis and his parents standing outside Uncle Vester's home in Tupelo, Mississippi, 1943.

161 Winfield Scott "Scotty" Moore III was born in Gadsden, Tennessee, on December 27, 1931. He was the youngest of five children.

162 Scotty Moore was born blind in one eye.

163 Delta Mae Presley, Elvis's aunt, married Patrick Biggs in the early 1930's.

164 Tom Parker met his future wife, Marie Mott Ross, through her father, a Spanish-American War veteran. Marie was one of six children.

165 Tom Parker and Marie Ross were married in Tampa, Florida, in 1932.

166 Raymond Barton Sitton, one of Elvis's bodyguards during the 1960's, was born in 1932.

167 In 1932, residents of Tupelo were asked to donate $1 each to build the North Mississippi Medical Center. Approximately $2,000 was raised from the 2,000 residents, which included the Presley and Smith families.

168 In December of 1932, Gladys Smith quit school and began a job at the Tupelo Garment Factory. She worked on the second floor.

169 Infamous outlaw Machine Gun Kelly robbed the Citizens State Bank in Tupelo in 1932. He got away with $17,000.

170 Before dating Vester and Vernon Presley, Gladys Smith dated Pid Harris and Rex Stamford. Rex proposed to Gladys, but she turned him down.

171 It was rumored that Gladys Smith had an affair with a married man, a local farmer who lived near her family's farm.

172 Vernon Presley initially dated Clettes Lee Smith while his brother, Vester, dated Gladys Love Smith. Gladys started dating Vernon instead because she thought Vester was too wild.

173 Gladys Smith first spotted Vernon Presley at Miller's Candy Store in April of 1933. It is rumored that Vernon and Gladys finally met at Roy Martin's Grocery Store in Tupelo in mid-1933. Vernon worked there as a delivery boy.

174 Gladys Smith lived on Kelly Street in Tupelo during the time she dated Vernon Presley. Their favorite place to go together was to the roller rink at the edge of Main Town.

175 After two short months of dating, Vernon Presley proposed to Gladys Smith. That same day, the couple eloped.

176 Marshall Brown had to loan Vernon Presley $3 for his and Gladys's marriage license.

177 Vernon Presley, Gladys Smith, Marshall Brown, and his wife, Vona Mae, hitchhiked to Pontotoc, Mississippi, twenty miles west of Tupelo, to get the marriage license for Vernon and Gladys.

178 Vernon Presley and Gladys Smith were married on Saturday, June 17, 1933, in Vernona, Mississippi, by Circuit Court Judge J. M. Gates.

179 Gladys Smith was 21 years old and Vernon Presley was 17 years old when they were married.

180 Marshall Brown and Vona Mae Pressley Brown were the legal witnesses to Vernon and Gladys Presley's marriage.

181 Vernon Presley's and Gladys Smith's families were shocked by the couple's elopement.

182 Vernon and Gladys Presley spent their wedding night at Marshall Brown's house.

183 After the wedding, the Presleys moved into Gladys's family's house on Berry Street in Tupelo.

184 After Gladys Smith married Vernon Presley, his sister, Gladys Earline, became known as "Little Gladys" so as not to confuse anyone.

185 After marrying Vernon Presley, Gladys picked cotton on Capp Shirley's land located on the Reese farm near Tupelo. She was paid $1.50 for every 100 pounds of cotton she picked.

186 In 1933, when Scotty Moore was two years old, his brother, Carney, worked at the Piggly Wiggly in Memphis and his brother Edwin joined the Navy.

187 George Nichopoulos, Elvis's doctor in the 1970's, was enrolled at Woodstock Grammar School in Alabama in 1933.

188 Vernon Presley was a milkman and a vegetable sharecropper on a dairy farm in Tupelo in 1934 and 1935.

189 The relationship between Gladys and Vernon's father, Jessie Pressley, was tense, in part because of the physical abuse Jessie had inflicted on Vernon as a teen.

190   Dominic Joseph "DJ" Fontana was born in 1934. He was Elvis's drummer in the 1950's.

191   After owning his own circus, Tom Parker became a press agent for carnivals, circuses, and showboats.

192   Samuel Presley was Vernon Presley's first cousin.

193   After a year of marriage, Gladys and Vernon Presley moved to Verona, Mississippi, which was located five miles from Tupelo down US Highway 45.

194   Gladys Presley dreamed of becoming a movie star and she idolized Clara Bow. Her family nicknamed her "Clara Bow" because of her outgoing personality.

195   Gladys Presley's family, the Smiths, lived on Luther Lummus's farm. They rented his property and worked as sharecroppers.

196   Gladys Presley often used snuff as a diet suppressant.

197   The Tupelo Garment Factory was located on South Green Street between Bluebell Alley and the railroad tracks in Milltown, Mississippi. Gladys Presley worked there from 1932 to 1938, where she earned $2.00 per 12-hour workday.

198   Singer sewing machines were used at the Tupelo Garment Factory when Gladys Presley worked there. In 1968, Singer sponsored Elvis's '68 Comeback Special.

199   During the 1930's, East Tupelo had only five streets.

200 Orville S. Bean, one of Vernon Presley's employers, was a dairy farmer who lived on Old Saltillo Road in Tupelo, Mississippi.

201 After a year and a half of living with other people, Vernon and Gladys Presley decided to build a house of their own. They borrowed $180 for building materials from Orville Bean, who was Vernon's boss at the time. Vernon and his brother, Vester, built a two-room shack on Old Saltillo Road.

202 The Presleys' 450 square foot shotgun shack at 306 Old Saltillo Road measured 15' x 30' and was not wired for electricity.

203 The Presleys' new home on Old Saltillo Road in Tupelo overlooked Mud Creek.

204 In May or June of 1934, Gladys and Vernon Presley found out that they were going to have a baby.

205 As Gladys Presley's pregnancy progressed, she guessed that she was carrying twins.

206 Another set of twins in the family were Gladys's cousins, Elzie and Ellis Mansell.

207 During her pregnancy, Gladys Presley stitched shirts together at the Tupelo Garment Factory.

208 In the wee hours of the morning of January 8, 1935, Gladys Presley went into labor at home and gave birth to twin boys.

209 It was raining hard in Tupelo, Mississippi, on January 8, 1935, the day that Elvis was born.

Vester and Clettes Presley, Elvis's uncle and aunt.
Vester was Vernon's older brother; Clettes was Gladys's younger sister.

210   Dr. William Robert Hunt, the local doctor, delivered Elvis Aron and Jesse Garon.

211   Elvis was Dr. William Hunt's 920th delivery.

212   Dr. William Hunt was 68 years old when he delivered Elvis.

213   There were two midwives on hand when Gladys gave birth to Elvis and Jesse: Faye Harris and Mrs. Edna Martin Robinson.

214   Faye Harris, one of the midwives present at the births of Elvis and Jesse Presley, was Gladys's schoolmate and the Presleys' neighbor on Old Saltillo Road. She also worked with Gladys at the Tupelo Garment Factory.

215   Jesse Garon Presley came into the world stillborn on Tuesday, January 8, 1935, at 4:05 a.m.

216   A rumor was started that Elvis's twin brother, Jesse Garon, died several hours after his birth.

217   Elvis Aron Presley was born on Tuesday, January 8, 1935, at 4:35 a.m.

218   Elvis's birth weight was a mere five pounds and he was 20 inches long.

219   Elvis was born with blue eyes and blonde hair.

220   Elvis had a scar on his back dating back to his birth.

221   Elvis's blood type was O positive.

222   The name Elvis comes from the Norse word "Alviss," which means "all wise."

223   The name "Alviss" was changed to "Elvis" by the French.

224   The name "Aaron" means "High Mountain" in Hebrew.

225   The name "Jessie" means "God's gift of grace" and is symbolic of wealth. "Garon" was a play on the name "Aaron." It is most often spelled "Garron," which means "guardian."

226   Faye Harris, a neighbor and co-worker of Gladys's who helped with the birth, was the person who inaccurately stated that Elvis was born first.

227   There were recorded births of twins on both sides of Elvis's family tree.

228   Rumor had it that Jesse Garon Presley was buried in a shoebox. Supposedly, Gladys tied a red ribbon around the box before burying him at Priceville Cemetery. The cemetery is located on Feemster Lake Road, three miles northeast of Tupelo.

229   It was rumored that Jesse Garon Presley was dressed in a baby blue outfit for his burial.

230   Because Vernon and Gladys Presley could not afford the $5 fee for a headstone, their son, Jesse, was buried in an unmarked grave.

231   It was and still is rumored that everyone in both Vernon and Gladys's families knew where Jesse Garon was buried. Elvis's rise to fame made them wary of theft, however, and therefore the location of the grave was kept a secret.

232   Due to the hardship of labor, Gladys Presley suffered constant hemorrhaging after the birth of her sons. At the urging of her friend, Mertice Finely, she allowed herself to be taken to the North Mississippi Family Medical Center located at 830 South Gloster Street, where she stayed for two weeks.

233   Brother Holly, the Pentecostal minister of the First Assembly of God Church, informed the Tupelo congregation of the birth of the Presley twins. He asked the congregation to help the family in any way they could.

234   The Presleys were Protestant.

235   It is said that both Gladys and Vernon liked First Assembly of God Church musical director Aaron Kennedy so much that they used his first name as Elvis's middle name.

236   It was reported that Gladys developed a nervous condition after Jesse Garon's death. She was constantly worried that Elvis would die as well; her worries were compounded by her husband's inability to get work and the family's lack of money.

237   In Great Britain, South Wales, just twenty miles from the Prescelly Mountains, is a town called St. Elvis.

238   Dr. William R. Hunt did not fill out Elvis's birth certificate until January 10, 1935.

239   On Elvis's birth certificate, Dr. William Hunt spelled Elvis's name "Ailvis Aaron."

240   Elvis's birth certificate incorrectly listed Gladys as a 21-year-old factory worker and Vernon as a 20-year-old laborer, as per Gladys's instructions.

241   On Jesse Garon's birth and death certificates, Dr. William Hunt misspelled Jesse's middle name as "Garion."

242   Dr. William Hunt listed "home" as the place of birth on Elvis's birth certificate.

243   Elvis's hospital ID number was IF-205-7B (M). A nurse took Elvis's footprints for hospital records.

244   Elvis was born with a web of skin between the second and third toes on his right foot. Later in his life, Elvis believed that it was a sign of being a twin.

245   When Dr. William Hunt discovered that the Presleys were unable to pay his $15 delivery fee, he billed the local welfare agency.

246   Elvis's astrological sign was Capricorn, the mountain goat. Elvis became intrigued by astrology and studied it in the 1970's. Capricorn is the sign of the architect of other people's dreams.

247   The element of the Capricorn, Elvis's sign, is the "Cardinal Earth."

248   According to astrology, Elvis's planetary influence was Saturn.

249   The body parts governed by Capricorn are the joints. Elvis had problems with his joints in his later years.

250   Elvis's colors, according to astrology, were brown, red, green, blue, and purple.

251   According to astrology, Elvis's jewels were the ruby, the garnet, and coral. His mystical jewel was the onyx.

252   Elvis's astrological/mystical musical key was A minor.

253   Elvis's compatible astrological signs were Taurus, Scorpio, and Virgo.

254   In numerology, Elvis was a 9.

255   According to numerology, some of the positive aspects of a number 9 include being bold, affectionate, charismatic, energetic, instinctual, and ambitious.

256   According to numerology, some of the negative aspects of a number 9 include being conceited, vulnerable, unorthodox, rebellious, excessive, and restless.

257   It was shortly after Elvis's birth that his parents spelled his name Elvis Aron. They unwittingly omitted the second "a" due to their lack of education.

258   Because of the Presleys' poverty, all of Elvis's baby things were given to Gladys by her friends at a baby shower.

259   Elvis was never circumcised.

260   The first time Elvis was taken to the First Assembly of God Church in Tupelo was just one month after he was born.

261   Gladys feared all kinds of storms. Whenever one hit Tupelo, she and Elvis hid in the cellar.

A pre-teen Elvis riding a bicycle near his family's house on Old Saltillo Road.

262   By 1935, there were several other Pressley families living near the Vernon Presleys: Goebel Pressley on Berry Street; Gordon, Jack, Sales, and Tennise Pressley on Kelly Street; and J.D. Pressley on Old Saltillo Road.

263   George Klein was born in 1935. He became Elvis's close friend.

264   WDIX was Tupelo's first radio station. The star disc jockey was Mississippi Slim. Elvis listened to WDIX when he lived in Tupelo.

265   Vernon Presley's brother, Vester, married Gladys Presley's sister, Clettes Lee Smith, in September of 1935. They had one child, a daughter named Patsy.

266   Vester Presley, Elvis's uncle, played the guitar at various country clubs, dances, and hoe-downs in and around Tupelo.

267   Gladys Presley's mother, Octavia, died of tuberculosis in 1935. She was buried alongside her husband Robert, who had died of pneumonia in 1933, at the Presbyterian Church in Spring Hill, Mississippi.

268   Charles Franklin Hodge was born in Decatur, Alabama, in 1935. He became Elvis's stage hand, musician, and backup singer.

269   In 1935, Max H. Furbringer was named chairman of the Memphis Municipal Housing Administration. His architectural company designed Graceland.

270   On January 1, 1936, Noah Pressley, Elvis's great uncle, became Mayor of East Tupelo.

271   Robert Gene West was born in 1936. Later known as "Red," he

became Elvis's first bodyguard in 1954. The two were long-time friends.

272   Desperate to feed his family, Vernon Presley stole food from a local grocery store. He was caught and had to spend a few days in jail.

273   The women of the Smith and Presley families occasionally gathered at Gladys Presley's house to put together jigsaw puzzles while they gossiped.

274   Ralph Moore, Scotty Moore's older brother, joined the Navy in 1936. Before Ralph left, he gave Scotty a guitar.

275   On April 5, 1936, a tornado ripped through Tupelo. Vernon, Gladys, Elvis, and Minnie Mae were at Noah Pressley's house huddled in a corner. The St. Mark's Methodist Church directly across the street from the Presley's Old Saltillo Road shack was blown to pieces, while the Presley's two-room home stood unscathed.

276   Alan Fortas was born April 6, 1936. Alan worked for Elvis as a member of his entourage in 1958. He was the nephew of Supreme Court Judge Abraham Fortas.

277   The Presleys owned an icebox in the late 1930's-early 1940's. Elvis and Gladys went to the ice plant every two or three days for ice.

278   Shortly after Elvis was able to walk and talk, his parents began taking him to the First Assembly of God Church, located at 206 Adams Street in Tupelo, on a regular basis.

279   During the time that the Presleys lived in Tupelo, there were four pastors at the First Assembly of God Church: Rev. Edward D. Parks,

Rev. James F. Ballard, Rev. Frank Smith, and, in 1937, Gladys Presley's uncle, Gains Mansell.

280   The First Assembly of God Church in Tupelo forbade all dances and movies. Even though the Presleys belonged to the church, they did not agree with nor abide by its policies and beliefs. Vernon and Gladys believed that music and entertainment were important.

281   As a child, Elvis's favorite food was Skippy peanut butter, which he loved to spread on crackers.

282   In order to feed his family, Vernon Presley sometimes went out hunting for squirrel.

283   In the late 1930's, Gladys Presley's brother, Travis Smith, married a woman named Lorraine. They had four sons: Robert, William, Eugene, and Carroll.

284   Gladys Presley's sister, Lillian, married Charles Mann sometime in the late 1930's. They had one son, Robert.

285   Martin Lacker was born in the South Bronx, New York, in 1937. He was a member of Elvis's entourage and served as one of the best men at Elvis and Priscilla's wedding on May 1, 1967.

286   Elvis began singing when he was just two years old.

287   On November 16, 1937, Vernon Presley, Travis Smith, and Luther Gable were arrested for forgery. Their employer, Orville Bean, reported the crime. The next day, the *Tupelo Journal* printed the story of the arrest.

288 On January 4, 1938, two bonds were posted in the State of Mississippi. C.E. Biggerstaff and J.H. Gable posted bond for Luther Gable and J.D. Pressley and J.G. Brown posted bond for Travis Smith. No bond was posted for Vernon Presley. Vernon's father thought that Vernon was a lazy good-for-nothing and believed that jail time would teach him a lesson. Both bails were set at $500.

289 When Elvis was three years old, he had a tricycle that he rode around his family's Old Saltillo Road house.

290 As a child, Elvis called milk "butch."

291 In the mid-1930's, Tupelo had three water wells. As the Presleys had no running water in their home, Elvis would go with his mother to the nearest well every day to fill a large bucket.

292 When Elvis was growing up in Tupelo, the railroad tracks between East Tupelo and West Tupelo belonged to the Mobile-Ohio line and the St. Louis-San Francisco Line.

293 While at the First Assembly of God Church, a three-year-old Elvis liked to run up to the choir and try to sing along.

294 Joseph Carmine Esposito was born in New York City in 1938. He became Elvis's right hand man, an important member of his entourage, and the other best man at Elvis's May 1967 wedding.

295 From the 1930's on, Gladys Presley permed her hair with Toni home permanents.

296 Some of the other families living in Tupelo, Mississippi, at the time Vernon and Gladys Presley lived there were the Adams, the

Archibalds, Mrs. Irma Bickerstaff, the Browns, the Cooks, the Flynns, the Griffins, the Longs, the Merchants, the Pitts, the Robbins, the Robinsons, the Rodgers, the Jessie D. Pressleys, the Noah Pressleys, and the T.E. Pressleys.

297 Red West's cousin, Delbert "Sonny" West, was born in 1938. He was one of Elvis's bodyguards.

298 On May 25, 1938, Vernon Presley was convicted of forgery. In November of 1937, Vernon, Travis Smith, and Luther Gable had sold Orville Bean a pig and then altered the amount of the check from $4 to $14.

299 Vernon Presley was incarcerated in the Lee County Jail after his arrest for forgery.

300 Vernon Presley was sentenced to three years in prison by Tupelo Superior Court Judge Thomas J. Johnston after he was found guilty of forgery.

301 When he was convicted of forgery in 1938, Vernon Presley was sent to Parchman Penitentiary, a brutal state prison located two hours from Tupelo. Parchman was on a 16,000 acre farm where the prisoners were forced to work every day. It was rumored that Vernon was whipped by prison guards, leaving scars on his back.

302 Gladys and Elvis visited Vernon at Parchman Penitentiary every weekend while he was incarcerated for forgery. F.L. Bobo, who would eventually become the manager of the hardware store where Elvis got his first guitar, drove Elvis and Gladys to the prison most weekends. When Bobo was unavailable, Elvis and Gladys took a Greyhound bus. The trip took five hours.

Milam Junior High School class photo.
Elvis is at far right, second row from top.

303 Vernon Presley served only nine months of his three year forgery sentence at Parchman Prison, from June 1, 1938, to February 6, 1939. Thanks to Gladys's petitioning, the judge let Vernon out early.

304 During Vernon Presley's incarceration, Gladys worked at Reed's Garment Company as a seamstress and lived with her cousin Frank and his family.

305 Later in life, Elvis recalled that while his father was in prison in 1938, he considered himself to be the head of the family even though he was only three years old.

306 Nancy W. Rooks was born in Fayette County, Tennessee, on August 8, 1938. She became Elvis's cook and maid at Graceland in 1966.

307 Vernon Presley developed a severe case of insomnia after his nine-month prison sentence for forgery.

308 Vernon Presley's first job after spending time in prison for forgery was at Leake and Goodlett Lumber Company, located at 105 East Main Street in Tupelo. He earned $18 a week.

309 As a child, Elvis preferred eating with a spoon rather than a fork. As the years passed, he used a spoon all the time and completely disregarded the fork.

310 Wallace E. Johnson was the president of Wallace E. Johnson Homes, Inc., located at 875 Rayner in Memphis. He and his wife, Alma, lived at 99 N. Century in Memphis. His company built the Lauderdale Courts in 1938. The Presleys lived there for a short time after moving to Memphis in 1948.

311 Wallace E. Johnson Homes Inc.'s vice presidents were Ernest McCool and John M. Fox.

312 Max H. Furbringer and Merrill Ehrman, of the firm Furbringer & Ehrman, teamed with Walk C. Jones to produce and design churches, courthouses, and schools in Memphis. Furbringer and Ehrman were architects working out of the 1004 Union Planters National Bank Building. Max H. Furbringer lived with his wife, Sophie, at 1437 Goodbar Avenue while Merrill G. Ehrman lived at 3824 Poplar Blvd. in Memphis.

313 Furbringer & Ehrman drew up the preliminary plans for the Graceland estate in 1938. Twelve buildings were erected on the 13.8-acre site.

314 In addition to Graceland, the Overton Park Shell in Memphis was designed by Furbringer & Ehrman, as was the roof garden of the Peabody Hotel. It was designed in a style reminiscent of the Tara plantation from *Gone With The Wind*.

315 Dr. Thomas D. Moore (b. April 11, 1883) and his wife, Ruth, hired Robert C. Crouch to build Graceland. Crouch was a general contractor whose business was located in the 703 Sterick Building. Finished in 1939, the estate was made of white Tishomingo stone, which is named after one of the two Indian-named creeks in Tupelo. The other creek was the Chipawa.

316 Thomas D. Moore, MD, the original owner of Graceland, was a urologist and surgeon who worked out of suites 102-10 in the Physicians & Surgeons Building, the annex to the Baptist Memorial Hospital, which was located at 899 Madison Avenue. His office telephone number was 5-3761.

317 At the time it was first built, Graceland's address was Graceland, US Highway 51 South, RD7 Box 789. The private home phone number of the owner, Dr. Thomas Moore, was 9-7083.

318 Robert C. Crouch (b. March 22, 1896), the general contractor who built Graceland, and his wife, Roxy L., lived at 374 Josephine in Memphis.

319 Graceland was once known as the Graceland Christian Church.

320 Graceland was also called Graceland Farms, and had its own blacksmith's shop.

321 Michael Stone was born in 1939. Mike had an affair with Priscilla Presley, which contributed to Elvis and Priscilla's divorce in 1972.

322 When Elvis was old enough to pay attention, his mother read him stories from the Bible every night.

323 Twin brothers Jerry and Terry Presley were reportedly Elvis's cousins.

324 In the late 1930's and early 1940's, one of Elvis's school buddies was Joseph Savery.

325 As a child, Elvis loved to eat bologna sandwiches. He savored every bite, knowing that bologna was a luxury his family could not often afford.

326 Gladys once threw groceries at a boy who was threatening to beat up Elvis.

327 Farley Guy was one of Elvis's best childhood friends.

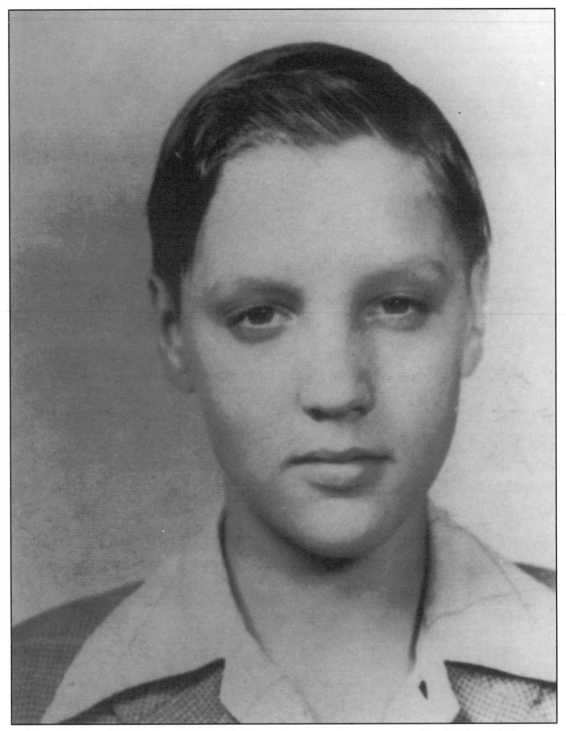

One of Gladys's favorite photos of Elvis, taken at Milam Junior High School in 1948.

328 It has been said that Vernon Presley had a good singing voice and sang often.

329 In 1939, when Elvis was only four years old, he ran away from home—but only for about 15 minutes!

330 The Presley family was so poor while they were living in Tupelo that they survived on vegetables most of the time.

331 Broadcast Music, Inc. (BMI), was formed by several radio broadcasters in 1939. Elvis's recordings were registered with this organization.

332 Marion Keisker, Sam Phillips' secretary at Sun Studios, divorced her husband and moved back to Memphis from St. Louis, Missouri, in 1939.

333 Elvis never allowed any of his friends inside his home at 306 Saltillo Road. He was embarrassed about the small size and shabbiness of the house.

334 Orville Bean evicted Vernon Presley and his family from their Old Saltillo Road home in May of 1939 because they could not repay the loan for building materials on the house. The Presleys moved in with Travis Smith and his family, who lived nearby.

335 In October 1940, Vernon moved his family in with his brother, Vester, and his wife, Clettes, on Reese Street. They stayed there for several months.

336 Elvis's two best friends in Tupelo were Guy Harris and Odell Clark. Guy Harris became a sergeant with the Tupelo police force.

337 In 1940, Vernon Presley worked for the Works Progress Administration (WPA), which was a part of Franklin D. Roosevelt's New Deal. By working for the WPA, Vernon Presley was exempt from military service.

338 In 1940, Sales Pressley worked with Vernon constructing public outhouses for the WPA in Pascagoula, Mississippi, located near Biloxi.

339 Priscilla (Beaulieu)Wagner's parents, Anne Iversen and James Wagner, met at a USO dance in 1940.

340 Elvis and his family lived with the Sales Pressleys in Pascagoula, Mississippi, for a period of seven months in 1940.

341 Elvis's great uncle, Noah Pressley, was the first person to take Elvis to the Tupelo Zoo and was the first to take him out to dinner in a restaurant.

342 Vernon Presley's uncle, Noah Pressley, ran a grocery store and drove a school bus.

343 As a child, Elvis nicknamed his mother "Baby."

344 An average weekly grocery bill for the Presleys in the 1940's was $15. At one time, Vernon and Gladys's combined incomes were only $35 per week.

345 The Presleys were well known throughout Tupelo as honest people. Friends lent them money without question, except as to when it would be paid back.

346 Elvis's voice was high pitched and off key when he was young. Many of his friends and relatives stated that it hurt their ears to listen to him.

347 As a child, Elvis called water "ducklin."

348 Tom Parker became the Florida Humane Society's field agent in the 1940's. Tom Parker has been credited with being the first person to invent the "pet cemetery," located behind the Florida Humane Society building on Armenia Avenue in Tampa.

349 Elvis nicknamed feet "sooties" as a child.

350 When the Grand Ole Opry came to Tampa as a tent show, Tom Parker was hired as the promoter.

351 Willie Whiteman was one of Elvis's cousins. His grandmother was Elvis's grandmother's sister.

352 As a child, Elvis never owned a pair of new shoes. He wore hand-me-downs and owned only one pair of shoes at a time.

353 In 1941, at the age of 32, Tom Parker worked as a dog catcher in Tampa, Florida.

354 In Tupelo in the mid-1940's, Reverend James Ballard was the pastor of the Presley's church.

355 The first broadcast of WELO Radio in Tupelo, Mississippi, was on May 15, 1941. This was Elvis's favorite radio station.

356 James Burton was born in Louisiana on August 21, 1941. He was Elvis's guitar player from 1969 to 1977.

357 Ed Parker, Elvis's karate instructor, learned karate from William Kwai Sun Chow in 1941.

358 In 1941, Vernon and his brother, Vester, worked at Long's Dry Cleaners, located at 130 East Main Street in Tupelo.

359 In the 1940's, Vernon entertained his family by playing the banjo.

360 Stillborn babies and early death were not uncommon in the Pressley-Smith families. Annie Pressley's daughter, Barbara Sue, died a few hours after birth in 1941.

361 James Ausborn was one of Elvis's best friends in Tupelo. He was Carvel Lee "Mississippi Slim" Ausborn's younger brother.

362 At the age of six, Elvis developed acute tonsillitis.

363 Vester Presley worked for C&E Cleaners in the early 1940's.

364 In the 1940's, Elvis was baby-sat by his cousin, Bobby Roberts.

365 As a young boy, Elvis loved to play marbles.

366 Elvis nicknamed his mother "Satnin'." The name came from a popular lard product.

367 There were children from 26 Presley families enrolled in the Tupelo school system in the 1940's.

368 In the 1940's, Vernon worked on a construction job in Como, Mississippi, located 73 miles from Tupelo. He rented an apartment there so he wouldn't have to travel every day.

369 In 1941, Sam Phillips dropped out of high school to help his family financially.

370 When Elvis started school in 1941, the Tupelo education system was rated one of the best in the state of Mississippi.

371 Elvis developed a fear of snakes after finding them under his bedsheets and in his home when he was a child.

372 Elvis entered first grade on September 15, 1941, just a few weeks before the United States entered World War II.

373 As a youngster, Elvis loved to eat bananas. One of his favorite foods was cornflakes with bananas.

374 In September of 1941, a six-year-old Elvis was enrolled at the East Tupelo Consolidated/Lawhon School located at 140 Lake.

375 During Elvis's enrollment at East Tupelo Consolidated/Lawhon School, the student body was comprised of approximately 700 children.

376 Gladys walked Elvis to and from school each day when he attended East Tupelo Consolidated/Lawhon School. It was a half-mile walk.

377 The principal at East Tupelo Consolidated/Lawhon School when Elvis enrolled was Mr. J.D. Cole.

378 Elvis sang "God Bless My Daddy," "Old Shep," and "Leaf on A Tree" for his classmates while at East Tupelo Consolidated/Lawhon School.

379 Laverne Farrar Clayton was a cafeteria worker at East Tupelo Consolidated/Lawhon School when Elvis was a student there.

A 15-year-old Elvis portraying a cowboy at the Fairgrounds.

380 Gladys forced her son to wear longjohns in the winter. Elvis hated them because they were "itchy and scratchy."

381 Rhetha Smith Loyd, Gladys's older sister, burned to death in October of 1941. While pouring oil into the stove, she spilled some on herself and caught fire.

382 Sometime between 1941 and 1943, Vernon Presley became a deacon at the First Assembly of God Church in Tupelo.

383 In the 1940's, Vernon Presley cooked hot dogs and bologna for the Tupelo Meat Packing Company and Vester Presley worked for Harrison's Dry Cleaners.

384 In 1942, Vernon Presley moved his family to Kelly Street in Tupelo, where they lived for over two years.

385 Some time in the spring of 1942, Gladys Presley became pregnant for the second time. After only a few weeks, however, she had a miscarriage and was hospitalized at Tupelo General Hospital for treatment. That same year, Gladys was hospitalized for stress, nervosa, and other ailments. A seven-year-old Elvis spent all the time he could at the hospital holding his mother's hand.

386 In 1942, Patricia Boyd was born to Mr. and Mrs. T.F. Boyd. She became one of Elvis's secretaries at Graceland.

387 During the time that the Presleys lived in Tupelo, the surrounding communities were Baldwyn, Nettleton, Saltillo, Shannon, Verona, and Guntown.

388 Elvis learned how to play the guitar when he was seven years old. He

learned several chords from his uncles, Vester and Johnny.

389 It has been said that when Elvis was a youngster and learned new chords on his guitar, he practiced for hours, sometimes until his fingers bled.

390 Sam Phillips married Rebecca Burns, his high school sweetheart, in 1942.

391 Sam Phillips worked as a disc jockey at WLAY Radio in Muscle Shoals, Alabama, in 1942 and for WMSL Radio in Decatur, Georgia, from 1942 to 1945.

392 Jessie D. Pressley deserted Minnie Mae Presley in 1942. He filed for divorce in 1946, stating that she deserted him on October 19, 1942.

393 In 1942, Eddy Arnold convinced Tom Parker to move to Nashville, Tennessee, where Parker continued to manage the singer.

394 When he grew old enough to carry a hammer, Elvis enjoyed hammering nails into the trees near his house.

395 Elvis went by himself to the First Assembly of God Church for revival meetings every Wednesday. He loved to learn new spiritual songs.

396 Elvis loved to eat "soakies" as a child—homemade cornbread soaked in buttermilk.

397 Elvis befriended Becky Martin while he was a student at East Tupelo Consolidated/Lawhon School. Becky's father, Roy, owned Roy Martin's Grocery Store/Ice Cream Parlor.

398 Elvis owned two pet dogs as a child: Woodlawn was a white dog with brown spots and Muffy Dee was a brownish-red dog.

399 In the 1940's, Elvis's favorite comic books were *The Adventures of the Lone Ranger*, *Hopalong Cassidy*, *Tarzan*, *Batman*, and *Superman*. He later became interested in *Captain Marvel* and *Captain Marvel, Jr.* When *Captain Marvel* and *Captain Marvel, Jr.* comics were discontinued, Elvis was devastated!

400 Wayne Ernest was one of Elvis's good friends at East Tupelo Consolidated/Lawhon School. They often traded comic books. Elvis also traded comic books with his cousin, Harold Loyd.

401 Elvis had his first fight at school in 1942. Unfortunately, he was not the winner, and he sported a rather handsome shiner for a few days afterward.

402 Vernon never took Elvis fishing or hunting or on any other father-son outings when Elvis was small.

403 Elvis hated snakes and used to hunt them as a child.

404 As youngsters, Elvis and his friends went skinny-dipping in the creek near his Tupelo home.

405 When Elvis was in elementary school, Gladys did not allow him to go to Roy Martin's Grocery Store/Ice Cream Parlor after school with other kids from the neighborhood. She worried about him and wanted him to be near her instead.

406 Two of Elvis's teachers at the East Tupelo Consolidated/Lawhon School in Tupelo were Mrs. Harvey Wilson and a Mrs. Bell.

407   Elvis found out about the "facts of life" from his mother in 1943.

408   Jerry Schilling was born in 1943. He was a member of Elvis's entourage.

409   William Smith was born to Travis and Lorraine Smith in 1943. Billy was Elvis's favorite cousin.

410   When he was a young boy, Elvis wanted to be a doctor.

411   In 1943, at the age of eight, Elvis began to wear glasses. He was very self-conscious about how he looked and did not allow anyone to take his photograph while he was wearing them.

412   Beginning in 1943, Elvis spent Saturday afternoons at the Lee County Courthouse, located on Court Street between Broadway and Green, watching WELO Radio's "Saturday Jamboree." The program was broadcast live from 1:00 to 4:30 p.m. The courthouse was built in 1904 and was the third to be built on the site after fire destroyed the first two.

413   In the 1940's, Charles Boren was the station manager at WELO Radio.

414   WELO Radio was broadcast from a building on South Spring Street in Tupelo. The station was located above the Black and White Dry Goods Store.

415   As a child, Elvis loved potato salad and often ate it as his main dish for dinner.

416   While living in Tupelo, Elvis saw movies at the Lyric Theater, located at the corner of Broadway and Court Streets. The manager at that time was John Grower. Originally built as an opera house in 1912, the building became the Comus Theater, then the Strand. It became the Lyric Theater in the 1930's.

417 In 1944, Elvis was baptized at the First Assembly of God Church in Tupelo by Reverend Frank Smith.

418 In 1944, at the age of nine, Elvis learned how to ride a bicycle. He was taught by his Aunt Nash, who was nine years older than Elvis.

419 On April 10, 1944, Elvis was on the radio for the first time. It was during WELO Radio's "Saturday Jamboree," broadcast from Tupelo.

420 In May of 1944, WELO Radio aired on AM 1490 for 18 straight hours. The broadcast featured music, news, sports, and weather.

421 The Memphis branch of the First Assembly of God Church, located at 960 South Third Street, was built in 1944. The Presleys visited this branch after moving to Memphis.

422 Reverend Donald L. Dunavent was the pastor of the First Assembly of God Church in East Heights-Tupelo.

423 Priscilla's parents, Anne Iversen and James Wagner, eloped to Pensacola, Florida, on August 10, 1944. Anne was 14 years old at the time, and James was 20.

424 Elvis hated the taste and smell of fish from the time he was a young boy. He would not allow anyone to cook it or eat it in front of him.

425 From 1945 to 1948, Vernon Presley worked delivering vegetables and groceries for L.P. McCarthy Wholesale House. He was paid $22.50 every week.

Elvis and his cousin, Gene Smith, posing for the camera at the Mississippi-Alabama Fairgrounds.

426 During Vernon Presley's employment at L.P. McCarthy, he earned an extra $12 a week by using their truck to transport moonshine during his off hours.

427 Elvis learned how to drive a car at the age of nine!

428 It was reported that Elvis first learned how to drive in the delivery truck that Vernon drove for L.P. McCarthy.

429 James Davis, an old carnival friend of Tom Parker's, served two terms as governor of Louisiana. Jimmie Davis was also a singer and performer and was inducted into the Country Music Hall of Fame in 1972. During his term as governor, he honored his friend by giving him the title of "Honorary Colonel."

430 Elvis did not like to have his picture taken when he was a child. He rarely posed for photographs, thus making it quite difficult to find pictures of him as a youngster.

431 Elvis was never treated to a birthday party when he was a child.

432 Priscilla Ann Wagner, Elvis's future wife, was born on May 25, 1945, in Sheepshead Bay, Brooklyn, New York.

433 Gladys Presley cooked mustard greens in the spring and turnip greens in the winter for dinner.

434 Gladys did not allow Elvis to go to the movies by himself until he was ten years old.

435 In 1945, it was reported that Elvis went to a local store to ask for a job as a delivery boy. He told the owner that he needed the job to help his family, but he was turned down because of his young age.

436 In 1945, Sam Phillips worked for WLAC Radio in Nashville, Tennessee.

437 On August 5, 1945, the Presleys moved to another house on Berry Street in Tupelo, and they liked the house so much that they decided to buy it. Vernon paid owner Orville Bean a $200 deposit on the $2,000 house. On August 18, the transaction was recorded in the county records as the home located on Lot 18, 19 - Block 2 - northeast quarter of 33 - township 9 - range 6 east on Berry Street.

438 The Presleys bought their groceries at Mayhorn's Grocery & Market in Tupelo.

439 Sam Phillips was the host of the "Songs of the West" show on WREC Radio in Memphis from 1945 to 1949. The program aired every day at 4:00 p.m. Phillips was at one time the engineer for the CBS network WREC Radio, which was broadcast from the Skyway Room of the Peabody Hotel in Memphis.

440 Some time in the late 1940's/early 1950's, Sam Phillips hosted the "Saturday Afternoon Tea Dance" on WREC Radio in Memphis.

441 Sam Phillips went to the Home of the Blues record store in Memphis and purchased all the records that other radio stations didn't want so he could play them on his show.

442 Before becoming Sam Phillips's secretary, Marion Keisker was "Miss Radio of Memphis" on WREC Radio. She hosted her own program, "Kitty Kelly."

443 Kathy Westmoreland was born in Texarkana, Arkansas, on August 10, 1945. She was Elvis's soprano backup singer from 1970 to 1977.

444 As a boy, Elvis ate hamburgers at Dudie's Diner, located just 3 miles from his house in Tupelo.

445 While a student at the Memphis College of Music, Dewey Phillips worked in the record department of the W.T. Grant Store located on Main Street.

446 In 1945, while in the eighth grade, Scotty Moore had to take a horse and buggy to get to school.

447 In 1945, Elvis's fifth grade teacher at East Tupelo Consolidated/ Lawhon School was Mrs. Oleta Bean Grimes, Orville Bean's daughter. She was born on April 17, 1911.

448 On October 3, 1945, Elvis entered the Mississippi-Alabama State Fair & Dairy Show talent contest. He won fifth place by singing his favorite song, "Old Shep." The fair, first held in 1904, started as the Lee County Fair.

449 Gladys and Vernon Presley went to many doctors in hopes of remedying their inability to have more children.

450 Vernon Presley once worked on the East Bottom Farm in Tupelo picking cotton, corn, and peas.

451 In November of 1945, Priscilla's father, James Wagner, was killed when the plane he was on crashed into a mountain during a snowstorm in Wingdale, New York.

452 In the mid-1940's, Bob Neal was a disc jockey for WMPS Radio located at 112 Union Avenue in Memphis. His program, "The Bob Neal Farm Show," aired every day from 5:00 to 8:00 a.m. Bob was one of Elvis's first managers.

453 As a child, Elvis enjoyed making snow ice cream. This concoction consisted of snow, sugar, and a touch of vanilla.

454 On Monday, January 7, 1946, a tornado hit Lee County. An eleven-year-old Elvis was terrified by the storm, as was his mother. They hid in the basement for hours until the twister passed. The Presley home was spared.

455 When Elvis was 11, he wanted a bike so that he could have a paper route. The $50 bicycle was far too expensive for the Presleys, so they bought their son a guitar instead.

456 For Elvis's birthday in 1946, Vernon and Gladys bought their son his first guitar and music book. Both gifts came from the Tupelo Hardware Store located at 114 West Main Street and owned by George C. Booth. The store manager was Forrest L. Bobo, who was born on October 2, 1901. According to Mr. Bobo, the guitar cost $7.75 plus two cents tax.

457 In 1946, Elvis's great uncle, Noah Pressley, became the marshal of Tupelo.

458 Scotty Moore quit school after the ninth grade and went into farming.

459 In 1946, Vernon Presley lost his job and was forced to sell the Berry Street house in Tupelo. His friend, Aaron Kennedy, bought the house for $3,000 on January 18, 1946.

460   The Presleys moved into a house on Commerce Street in Tupelo for a short time in mid-January of 1946.

461   Minnie Mae Presley first moved in with Elvis and his parents in 1946 when they lived on Commerce Street in Tupelo.

462   Between 1946 and 1948, Elvis sang outside the Tupelo Hotel located on Spring Street. Passersby gave him nickels, dimes, and quarters, marking the first time that Elvis was paid to perform.

463   Elvis won a Bible for singing at his church when he was eleven years old. He kept this Bible until his death in 1977.

464   Many members of the Smith and Presley families said that Elvis got his rhythm from his mother.

465   In June of 1946, Elvis's class became the final group of students to graduate from the East Tupelo Consolidated /Lawhon School before Tupelo and East Tupelo merged.

466   In 1946, Joseph Coughi and John Angelo Novarese (b. November 13, 1923) opened the Popular Tunes Record Store at 306 Poplar Avenue in Memphis. Elvis bought many albums from this store. In 1956, Joseph Cuoghi founded Hi Records, which later went on to include recording artists such as Al Green, Bill Black, and Willie Mitchell. Cuoghi lived at 515 E.H. Crump Blvd. E in Memphis.

467   Elvis was enrolled at Milam Junior High School in September of 1946. The school was located at 720 West Jefferson in Tupelo.

468   Elvis was one of fifteen children in his homeroom during his first year at Milam Junior High in Tupelo.

Minnie Mae Presley, Elvis's paternal grandmother.

469 One of Elvis's sixth grade teachers at Milam Junior High was Mrs. Quay Webb Camp, who was born on June 28, 1903. Some of his other teachers included Essie Patterson (b. August 18, 1899), Mrs. Montrose Tapscott, and Ms. Virginia Plumb.

470 One of Elvis's classmates at Milam Junior High in Tupelo was Billy Welch, who became a psychiatrist. Elvis and Billy played instruments and sang together in the school basement during lunch breaks.

471 Ronald Tindall, Donald Williams, and Raymond McCraig were some of Elvis's friends from Milam Junior High in Tupelo.

472 Patricia Medford and Karen Pritchard were two of Elvis's cousins.

473 As a student at Milam Junior High in Tupelo, Elvis entered a talent show and lost. The contest was held at the Emma Edmonds Auditorium.

474 Some of Elvis's classmates at Milam Junior High School in Tupelo admitted inviting Elvis to their parties so they could make fun of him because he was different.

475 One of Elvis's classmates at Milam Junior High was Evelyn Helms. Her mother worked at the Tupelo Garment Factory with Elvis's mother.

476 In the 1940's, Elvis was elected to the Milam Junior High School student council.

477 Leroy Green, Jr. was one of Elvis's friends at Milam Junior High in Tupelo. He and Elvis were the two poorest students enrolled at the school.

478 The East Tupelo Consolidated School was renamed Lawhon Elementary School after Elvis enrolled at Milam Junior High School (1946/47).

479 In the mid-1940's, Elvis's uncle, Vester Presley, worked on a farm operated by Patrick and Velma Dougherty on Old Saltillo Road in Tupelo.

480 When he was ten years old, Elvis and several of his friends worked in a cotton field where they were paid $1 for half a day's work. After approximately two weeks, Elvis and his pals quit because they decided the pay was too low.

481 Scotty Moore quit his farming job in 1947 and went back to school, where he enrolled in the tenth grade.

482 Some time in early 1947, the Presleys lived at 510 1/2 Maple Street with Gladys's cousin, Frank Richards (b. October 27, 1895), his wife Leona, and their daughter, Corrine.

483 While living in the Richards family home, the Presleys could not afford to pay for room and board, so Gladys cleaned her cousin's house and baby-sat the children in lieu of payment.

484 In early 1947, Gladys Presley, who hated being a homemaker, went to work for the Mid-South Laundry. Elvis began sporting crisply pressed shirts and pants to school every day.

485 Ed Parker was first exposed to the martial art of Kempo in 1947, when he was 16 years old. Parker became Elvis's Kempo instructor.

486 In 1947, Jessie D. Pressley, Elvis's grandfather, worked at the Pepsi-Cola bottling plant in Tupelo.

487 In June of 1947, Vernon Presley moved his family to a house on Mulberry Street in Tupelo. The Presleys hated the area, known as "Mobile Alley," which was located near the city dump and the fairgrounds.

488 Elvis became friends with the Crabb brothers, who lived next door to the Presleys in "Mobile Alley" in Tupelo.

489 As a pre-teen, Elvis called girls "punks."

490 When Elvis was 12 years old, he borrowed the book *Told by Uncle Remus* by Joel Chandler Harris from the Milam Junior High School library, as evidenced by his signature on the library card, stamped November 20, 1947.

491 In January of 1948, Scotty Moore joined the US Navy. His status was Fireman III. During his time with the Navy, he received one Chinese and one Korean service medal.

492 Scotty Moore put together a band while he was in the Navy, known as The Happy Valley Boys.

493 In 1948, East Tupelo and Tupelo merged. The distance between the two towns was one mile.

494 In 1948, the Presleys moved to what was considered to be the worst part of Tupelo, an area called "Shakerag." Their house, located at 1010 North Green Street, was near a slaughterhouse and was owned by Dr. James Green. Although the Presleys had moved to a bad area, many people considered them middle class because they were living in a doctor's house. This was their last home in Tupelo.

L.C. Humes High School library workers, 1949. Elvis is at far right, top row.

495 When the Presleys moved to the "Shakerag" area of Tupelo, they befriended a black man named John Allen who owned a grocery store located 100 yards from the Presleys' home.

496 As a boy, Elvis loved to eat Milky Way candy bars.

497 In 1948, Gladys Presley worked as a sewing machine operator for a company called Fashion Curtains.

498 On February 19, 1948, Gladys took Elvis to the public library in Tupelo to fill out a library card application.

499 Anne Iversen Wagner met Joseph Beaulieu at New London Junior College in the spring of 1948.

500 A divorce between Minnie Mae Presley and Jessie D. Pressley, Elvis's paternal grandparents, was granted in 1948 after Minnie Mae wrote to the judge explaining her side of the story. The divorce did not offer alimony or a settlement to either party.

501 Judge Lawrence Speckman granted the divorce between Jessie D. Pressley and Minnie Mae Presley. On the court papers granting their divorce, Jessie signed his name "Pressley" and Minnie Mae signed hers "Presley."

502 Jessie D. Pressley remarried in 1948 and moved to Kentucky. His second wife, Vera Kennard Pruitt, was a school teacher.

503 Until the Presleys moved to Memphis, Elvis had never seen a bathroom inside a house.

504 Earl K. Long, Governor of Louisiana in 1948 and younger brother of the infamous Huey Long, was another governor that bestowed the honorary title of "Colonel" upon Tom Parker.

505 RCA-Victor introduced 45 rpm records in 1948.

506 When Elvis was 13 years old, his parents bought him a bicycle. After he fell off the bike and broke his arm, he had to give the bicycle away.

507 Ed Sullivan's *Toast of the Town* show began airing as a weekly series on June 20, 1948. Elvis appeared on this famous CBS-TV show in 1956.

508 Anne Iversen Wagner, Priscilla's mother, married Joseph Paul Beaulieu in Groton, Connecticut, on September 11, 1948.

509 Just after the Presleys moved to Memphis, Gladys's sister, Lillian, and her family moved into the 1010 North Green Street house in Tupelo.

510 When the Presleys moved to Memphis in September of 1948, they sold all of their furniture to relatives and friends.

511 The Presleys moved to Tennessee on September 12, 1948, driving the 105 miles from Tupelo to Memphis on Highway 78 in Vernon's green 1939 Plymouth.

512 The Presleys' first home in Memphis was located at 370 Washington Street. Next door was a vegetable stand called "Magolio."

513 After settling in Memphis, the Presleys became members of the Assembly of God Church located at 1085 McLemore.

514 Vernon and Gladys enrolled Elvis in the Christine Public School located at 285 N. 3rd Street on November 8, 1948. Elvis went there for a year to finish the eighth grade.

515 Elvis's teacher at the Christine Public School was Ms. Conyers.

516 The principal of the Christine Public School when Elvis attended was Mrs. Margaret Walker who lived at 164 Market Street.

517 Other teachers at the Christine Public School at the time Elvis attended were Annie M. Johnson (417 Edith Ave.), Rubie M. McNicholas (591 N. Trezevant), Nell R. Silk (1328 Mississippi Blvd.), Priscilla Phillips (2184 Cowden Ave.), and Elizabeth Watson (148 Stonewall, Apt. 2).

518 Elvis received an "A" in language and "C's" in music and science when he attended the Christine Public School in Memphis.

519 Elvis was absent from school for 15 days in the eighth grade.

520 From the eighth grade on, Elvis brought his guitar to school every day.

521 In late September of 1948, Elvis and his family moved into an apartment located at 572 Poplar Avenue in Memphis. The building was owned by Clifton and Mildred Johnson who lived at 2971 Calvert. Clifton was a laborer at the Rotary Lift.

522 At 572 Poplar Avenue, where Elvis lived with his parents and Minnie Mae Presley, there was no Apartment #13, as it was considered bad luck. The building tenants and their apartment numbers were:
#1—the Presleys
#2—Milton Spellings (a sheetmetal worker) and wife Vera
#3—Ellis W. DeBerry (a router for RY Express) and wife Doris

#4—empty

#5—Mrs. Eugene Beise (widow of J.T.)

#6—Clarence McCollum and wife Dorothy

#7—empty

#8—Henry Coulter (roofer) and wife Rachel

#9—Aubrey Millican (sheetmetal worker at Skaggs Mfg. Co.)
      and wife Catherine

#10—Robert Cox (offbearer at Nickey Bros.) and wife Dell

#11—Nash Vallery

#12—Mrs. Lola Carpenter (widow of Albon)

#14—Mary Baker

#15—Mrs. Ruth Cox (widow of Frank)

#16—Willard Oldham and wife, Molly

#17—Barney Ashburn (carpenter) and wife Mozelle

#18—James Birmingham

523 The Poplar Avenue house the Presleys moved into in 1948 had once been a luxurious single family home. The Johnsons rented out rooms in the house for $35-$50. By the time the Presleys moved in, there were fifteen families living in the house, for a total of 60 people.

524 The Presleys lived in one room on the main level of the Poplar Avenue house in Memphis and paid $35 a month in rent. Gladys was forced to cook meals on a hot plate because there was no stove or kitchen in the house.

525 A short while after the Presleys moved in, Tressie Miller, also from Tupelo, moved to an apartment right below the Presleys at 572 Poplar Avenue.

526 One of Elvis's boyhood dreams was to become a policeman.

527 Elvis had a difficult time making friends with white children when he first arrived in Memphis. He eventually made several friends of the black children in the area.

528 When Elvis was 14 years old, Vernon and Gladys were on welfare.

529 Davada "Dee" Elliott married William Stanley in Camp Pickett, Virginia on February 1, 1949, right after William got a divorce from his first wife.

530 William Stanley was reportedly part Cherokee Indian and served as General Patton's bodyguard during World War II.

531 Mrs. Dell Taylor opened Taylor's Restaurant in 1949. It was located next door to the Memphis Recording Service/Sun Studios. Elvis often ate there while recording at the studio.

532 In early 1949, Vernon Presley worked in a candy factory. He eventually hurt his back and was forced to quit.

533 By the time Ed Parker was a senior at Kamehameha High School in the Kalihi district of Hawaii in 1949, he was already a black belt in karate.

534 Beginning in 1949, Vernon Presley sent his mother, Minnie Mae, $10 a month as his way of taking care of her.

535 In 1949, Bernard and Guy Lansky, sons of a Polish immigrant grocer, opened their first store on Beale Street in Memphis. Lansky's would eventually become Elvis's favorite clothing store.

536 On June 17, 1949, the Presley family was interviewed by Mrs. Jane Richardson, an advisor from the Memphis Housing Authority. On that

*L.C. Humes High School principal Thomas Brindley and his assistant
look over Elvis's photo in the 1953 yearbook.*

day, the Presleys qualified for financial assistance from the city. Mrs. Richardson was born on December 26, 1888, and lived at 6 S. McLean Blvd., Apt. 705.

537 Elvis met JD Sumner for the first time at a church songfest in 1949. JD and the Sunshine Boys were performing at the church; Elvis complimented JD after the show.

538 Shortly after meeting JD Sumner, Elvis auditioned for the gospel singing group The Songfellows. JD told Elvis that he did not have a good voice and should forget about a career in the music business. It's lucky for JD that Elvis didn't hold a grudge—in the 1970's, Elvis hired JD and his Stamps Quartet as his backup group!

539 During the late spring of 1949, Elvis and his family lived on Adams Street in Memphis for a short while.

540 Before the Presleys moved into apartment 328 at the Lauderdale Courts, Joseph Massey lived there. Joseph Massey was a masseur at Sadie Britt and, in 1950, moved to 183 S. Main Street.

541 Vernon, Gladys, and Elvis moved into the Lauderdale Courts on September 20, 1949. Minnie Mae Presley moved in with them as well, having left her home in West Point, Mississippi.

542 The Lauderdale Courts consisted of an I-shaped building with 430 apartments. It was located at Winchester Avenue, Third and Lauderdale Streets in Memphis. The building took up half the block, running from the Wolf River to 300 N. Main Street.

543 The Lauderdale Courts, although situated in only one building, had several different street addresses: 441-89 Alabama Avenue, 180-265

Market Mall, 182-314 Exchange, 240-288 N. 3rd, 219-52 Hill, 183-231 Winchester Avenue, and 234-90 N. Lauderdale.

544 The Lauderdale Courts, nicknamed "Pinchgut," was considered the Irish ghetto of Memphis.

545 The Presleys lived in the 327-335 section of the Lauderdale Courts, which contained 66 apartments. To get to their apartment, you walked in the front door and turned right.

546 Before settling his family into apartment 328 at the Lauderdale Courts, Vernon filled out a Housing Authority form, stating that "...wall around the bathtub needs repair—apartment in need of paint job—1 shade will not roll in bedroom—light in front hall will not stay on—oven door will not shut tight—one leg of dresser broke off—bathroom sink stopped up—faucet in kitchen sink needs repair."

547 The Presleys paid $30 a month in rent for their Lauderdale Courts apartment, which consisted of two bedrooms, a living room, a bathroom, and a kitchen that was painted beige.

548 The Presleys did not have a telephone at the Lauderdale Courts.

549 While living at the Lauderdale Courts, Elvis suffered from sleepwalking. To prevent him from walking outside and possibly getting hurt, Gladys and Vernon removed all of the doorknobs in the apartment at night.

550 Other tenants living in the 185 Winchester Avenue section of the Lauderdale Courts were:
#327 - Mrs. Gladys Hunter (hosiery saleswoman at Lowenstein's Dept. Store)
#328 - the Presleys

#329 - Alvin McClure (clerk at Sainberg's Dry Goods) and wife Jamie

#330 - Mrs. Mildred Love

#331 - John J. Gallo (manager of Pan Am Service Station) and wife Edith

#332 - Carl Allen and wife, Fanny

#333 - Kathy L. Masters (secretary at John B. Goodwin Realty)

#334 - Mrs. Ruby Dougher

#335 - Charles Holmes (elevator operator) and wife Eola

551 Some of the Presleys' other neighbors at the Lauderdale Courts were Mrs. Mary Guy, Mrs. Sophie Foote, the Wilson family, the Wardlow family, and Doris Swersberry.

552 Caroline Turley and her mother, Mrs. Louise Turley, lived in the 189 Winchester wing of the Lauderdale Courts.

553 The Housing Authority of Memphis had its headquarters at 264 N. Lauderdale and their telephone number was 8-6841.

554 Joseph A. Fowler and Walter M. Simmons were the associate executive directors of the Memphis Housing Authority at the time the Presleys lived at the Lauderdale Courts.

555 One of the Presleys' best friends at Lauderdale Courts was Ruby Black (b. February 9, 1903), who was Bill Black's mother. Bill's younger brother, Johnny, who was three years older than Elvis, became one of Elvis's good friends.

556 Elvis did the laundry for his mother while living at the Lauderdale Courts.

557 Bill Black quit high school at the age of sixteen in order to play bass in Pappy's Polk Country Band at night. He was later forced to get another job to supplement his income, and worked at the Railway Express Agency during the day.

558 Minnie Mae Presley took her grandson with her to the Poplar Street Mission to pray. Reverend Jesse J. Denson (b. January 8, 1898) was the preacher and musician.

559 Gladys begged Reverend Denson of the Poplar Street Mission to give Elvis guitar lessons. He agreed, and the lessons were conducted in the laundry room at the Lauderdale Courts.

560 Jesse J. Denson was later affiliated with the Golden Rule Missionary Baptist Church located at 195 S. Manassas. At that time, he lived at 227 Winchester in Memphis.

561 Elvis frequented the Teen Canteen, one of the hot spots in Memphis. The club was located near the Lauderdale Courts.

562 Elvis enjoyed playing football with his friends and neighbors on the front lawn of the Lauderdale Courts, which was a large, grass-covered triangle.

563 Elvis played football at the Lauderdale Courts with a 17-year-old Billy Fletcher, who went on to set records at Memphis State University and play for the Denver Broncos.

564 Elvis and his friends hung out at the Lauderdale Courts Recreation Hall in the evenings and on weekends.

565 Elvis and his friends swam at the Malone swimming pool.

566 One of Elvis's good friends in Memphis was Mack Gurley.

567 Jim Denson lived at the Lauderdale Courts at the same time as the Presleys. He and Elvis became good friends, and stayed friends after Elvis became famous. Jim was an electrician who lived at 227 Winchester Avenue, Apt. E.

568 Elvis and his family shopped at the A. Schwab's Dry Goods Store, located at 163 Beale Street. It was owned and operated by the Schwab brothers, each of whom was an officer of the corporation. President Samuel Schwab and his wife Gertrude lived at 675 S. Barksdale; vice president Leo L. Schwab and his wife Beatrice lived at 683 S. Barksdale; 2nd vice president Abram J. Schwab and his wife Fannie lived at 1718 Lawrence Place; secretary/treasurer Elias O. Schwab and his wife Camille lived at 1934 Higbee.

569 The saleswomen at A. Schwab's were Mrs. Lucinda Blackburn, who lived at 272 Hernando, and Jo Ann Clark, who lived at 395 East Trigg Ave.

570 Businesses situated immediately adjacent to A. Schwab's were Epstein's Loan Office at 162 Beale Street and Memphis World News at 164 Beale Street.

571 The Presleys were so poor while living at their Lauderdale Courts apartment that they stocked up on eggs, bacon, and Pepsi-Cola whenever they had a bit of extra money. This would ensure them meals and drinks during leaner times.

572 While at the Lauderdale Courts, Elvis collected comic books. He had a metal shelf in his home on which he arranged his precious collection both alphabetically and by category.

One of Elvis's favorite teachers from L.C. Humes High School, Mrs. Mildred Scrivener.

573 Both Elvis and Vernon enjoyed fixing and playing with cars. They often dirtied their best clothes while working, and thought nothing of it.

574 In 1949, Vernon was hospitalized for a back ailment.

575 Elvis enrolled at L.C. Humes High School in late September of 1949.

576 Mrs. Billy Arnold was the registrar at L.C. Humes High School when Elvis enrolled at the school in 1949.

577 L.C. Humes High School was originally called the North Side High School. It was renamed in honor of Laurence Carl Humes, President of the Memphis Board of Education from 1918 to 1925.

578 When Elvis enrolled at L.C. Humes High School it was an all-white school with a student body of 1,600. The three story, red brick building is located at 659 North Manassas Street.

579 Thomas C. Brindley (b. February 7, 1893) was the principal of L.C. Humes High School when Elvis was a student there. He lived at 1505 S. Wellington with his wife, Ella.

580 Eleanor Richmond (b. August 10, 1903) was the assistant principal at L.C. Humes High School when Elvis enrolled there. She lived at 1780 Forrest.

581 Rose Ellen Blunt, who lived at 3611 Coleman, was the principal's secretary at L.C. Humes High School when Elvis enrolled there.

582 Elvis's L.C. Humes High School homeroom teacher in 1949 was Ms. Susan Johnson. Her classroom was number 224.

583 Elvis's ninth grade music teacher at L.C. Humes High School, Elsie Marmann (b. September 17, 1892), who lived at 289 Gaston Avenue, turned Elvis down when he tried out for the Glee Club. She told him that the Glee Club didn't need his kind of voice.

584 Helen Lochrie, who lived at 1394 Harbert Avenue, was Elvis's speech and drama teacher at L.C. Humes High School.

585 Elvis's transcript was transferred from Milam Junior High to L.C. Humes High School in October of 1949.

586 Other teachers at L.C. Humes High School when Elvis was enrolled there were:

Jennifer "Jennie" Allensworth (1102 Linden Ave. - Apt. 1)

Zula Boswell (125 N. Evergreen)

Roy Coats (1540 Forrest Ave.)

Mrs. Katie B. Conyers (991 Forrest Ave.)

Mary B. Fisher (443 Angelus)

Agnes Gibson (704 Inez)

Flois Gwaltney (174 S. Barksdale)

Katherine R. Hall (14 S. McLean Blvd. - Apt. 14)

Virginia Harrell (3260 Spottswood)

Rev. Amos B. Harrison (1109 Rozelle)

Walter S. Hiltpold (764 Cypress Dr.)

Mary Hurt (1786 Carr)

Susie M. Johnson (1259 Agnes Pl.)

Gladys Keathley (470 N. Garland)

Mary F. Kennedy (20 S. Evergreen)

Ardie L. Little (1394 Harbart Ave.)

Helen Lochrie (1394 Harbart Ave.)

Jimmie A. Meeks (2622 Fillmore Ave.)

Louise N. Moffet (1930 Lyndale Ave.)

Sue Patton (23 S. Pauline - Apt. 404)

Loriece M. Pearce (1866 Crump Ave.)

Dorothy E. Pierce (233 Garland - Apt. 3)

Keathley Presgrove (1689 Galloway Ave.)

Mabel H. Reed (330 N. Willet)

Lyde Robinson (765 Leath)

Mildred Scrivener (2989 Spottswood Ave.)

John B. Shelby (592 Bethel Ave.)

Mrs. Julia S. Stephens (35 E. Norwood)

Mrs. Henry Taylor (554 Eastern Dr.)

L. Buford Taylor (737 N. Merton)

Margaret Thompson (1532 Carr)

Mary Walker (132 Bellevue Blvd.)

Louise Weaks (129 W. Belvedere Blvd.)

587 Annie M. Prescott was an office secretary at L.C. Humes High School in the late 1940's to early 1950's. She lived at 632 N. Dunlap in Memphis.

588 Mrs. Mary C. Spencer was the cafeteria manager at L.C. Humes High School. She lived at 1764 Jackson Avenue in Memphis.

589 G.D. Musgraves, who lived at 1745 S. Trezevant, and James H. Walters of 1321 Lambert, were employees of the L.C. Humes High School in the early 1950's.

590 Nellie M. Ward was the maid at L.C. Humes High School in the 1940's and 1950's. She lived at 697 Wright in Memphis.

591 One of Elvis's best friends at L.C. Humes High School was Evan "Buzzy" Forbes, who was the freshman class president. Elvis and Buzzy were in the same second period biology class.

592 Elvis met George Klein at L.C. Humes High School in 1949.

593 Elvis befriended Jesse Georges at L.C. Humes High School.

594 Elvis feared that the kids at L.C. Humes High School would laugh at what he called his "ghetto slang," but he still did everything within his power to be noticed.

595 Elvis worked as a volunteer in the library at L.C. Humes High School when he was in the tenth grade. The position was given to students as a reward for good behavior, and Elvis was thrilled by the honor. Mrs. Flois Gwaltney was the librarian who worked with Elvis and other students, including Richard Flaniken, Billy Barber, George Makrus, Joe Coyle, Geraldine Barber, Herbert Blooming, Larry Holmes, Ralph Shinbaum, Charles Catros, Val Crotts, Charlotte Young, Doris Varnavas, Ruth Mandelman, Joyce Beard, Billie May Chiles, Louise Carson, Lillian Davis, Joan Liberts, Rachel Maddox, Joe Collins, Maureen Kapell, Nina Faverty, Jane Garey, Peggy Simmons, Norma Banks, Annie Varnavas, Billie Banks, and Evelyn Hicks.

596 While at L.C. Humes High School, Elvis loved to eat the school's sloppy joes and their spaghetti and meatballs.

597 While in high school, Elvis signed his name Elvis aron Presley. According to handwriting analysts, Elvis left the "a" in lower case to allow room for a capital "G," in honor of his dead brother's middle name.

598 Gladys Presley worked as a nurse's aide at St. Joseph's Hospital, located at 264 Jackson Avenue, from 1949 to 1952. Her duties included making beds, washing floors, and bathing patients. She earned four dollars a day, or fifty cents an hour.

599   From 1949 to 1953, Vernon Presley worked at the United Paint Company, located at 345 Jackson Avenue in Memphis. The company's telephone number was 8-4294 and the owners were Allen P. Redd, Winfred J. Huettel, William Wilkinson, and O. Marcus Laughlin. Vernon packed paint cans into crates and onto delivery trucks for 83¢ an hour. He earned approximately $33.50 a week.

600   Allen Redd, one of the owners of United Paint Company, and his wife, Mary E., lived at 1279 Sledge Avenue. The company had four other branches, located at 533 S. Highland, 245 E. McLemore, 1634 Union Avenue, and 446 Concord Avenue.

601   United Paint Company's manager was Murial Massey, who lived at 364 S. Somerville, Apt. 19. The clerk was Mrs. Myrtle Ryan, who lived at 1812 Poplar Avenue, Apt. 14.

602   Ed Parker went to Brigham Young University in Provo, Utah, in 1949. He became Elvis's Kempo instructor.

603   From late 1949 to early 1950, Elvis saw movies at the Rialto Theater located at 983 Jackson Avenue in Memphis. The manager of the theater at that time was James C. Augustine.

604   Minnie Mae Presley, Elvis's grandmother, liked to drink alcohol. She hid mini-bottles in her bags and pockets and sipped from them when she thought no one was looking.

605   John Angelo Novarese, the manager of the Popular Tunes Record Shop, located at 306 Poplar Avenue in Memphis, waited on Elvis when he visited the shop. John lived with his wife Helen at 484 Poplar Avenue, Apt. 11.

The L.C. Humes High School R.O.T.C. class photo. Elvis is circled.

606 In the late 1940's/early 1950's, a 45 rpm record sold anywhere from 59¢ to 89¢.

607 Brothers Jean and Julian Aberbach opened their first music publishing house in Berlin, Germany, in 1949. They went on to work with Elvis and RCA-Victor.

608 On December 30, 1949, Priscilla's half-brother, Donald Paul, was born.

609 In 1949, Vernon Presley's income was $2,080.

610 Elvis's favorite TV show in the early 1950's was *The Lone Ranger*, starring Clayton Moore. It ran on ABC from 1949 to 1957.

611 These were the Presleys listed in the Memphis Polk Directory for the year 1950, along with their home addresses and listed occupations:
Aaron O. & Jannie Presley, 1147 Biltmore, watchmaker
Albert & Dorothy Presley, 1474 Kyle, cook at the Kennedy Hospital
Albert & Georgia Presley, 1335 Arkansas, driver
Alex & Tennie Presley, 1474 Kyle, helper
Annie M. Presley, 658 Baltic, widow of William R.
Barron S. & Mai Presley, 1095 Faxon Ave.
C.V. Presley, 1481 S. Lauderdale, supervisor at Burdsal Adv. Dist.
Dorothy, 2656 Supreme, helper at Arthur H. Edington
Eugene & Leona Presley, 115 South Parkway W., owners of gas
    stations located at 404 E. Calhoun Ave. and 8 South Parkway E.
Gordon & Pernie Presley, 672 S. Camilla - Apt. D, driver
Harold E. & Bernice Presley, RD9 Box 1460, steelworker at Tri-
    Iron Works
Henry L. Presley, 1782 Evelyn Avenue, student
Henry S. & Ora L. Presley, 1782 Evelyn Avenue, cashier
Herman R. & Dorris Presley, 2197 S. Wellington, printer at Tri-State Press

Hobson C. & Annie Presley, 267 E. Olive, operator

Hubert P. & Stella M. Presley, 2475 Yale Avenue, repairman

Ida Presley, 127 Strahorn Avenue

Isabella Presley, 1651 Rayburn Boulevard, widow of Robert

James R. & Elsie Presley, 271 E. Trigg Avenue, clerk

James S. & Annie M. Presley, 366 South Parkway East, engineer
  at ICRR

J. Wade & Mary A. Presley, 1163 Biltmore, instructor at South
  college-watchmaking

Joseph W. Presley Jr., 1163 Biltmore, student

Leona Presley, 684 Ayers, dishwasher

Lewis A. Presley, 712 East, clerk

M. Herman & Veora H. Presley, 782 Atlantic, personnel assistant,
  Memphis General Depot

Mattie Presley, 258 W. Utah, maid at Link's Studio

Mignon Presley, 1207 Dorothy Place, stewardess

Minnie M. Presley, 572 Poplar Avenue Apt. 1, widow of J.D.

O. Virgil Presley, 1481 S. Lauderdale, supervisor at Burdsal Adv. Dist.

Robert A. & Flora Presley, 1136 Patton - Apt. 2, engineer at ICRR

Ruby Presley, 673 Somerville Mall - Apt. H

Vernon & Gladys Presley, 185 Winchester - Apt. 328, laborer

Virgil C. & Estelle Presley, 1481 S. Lauderdale, salesman

Virginia Presley, 712 East, widow of William L.

Vivian Presley, 558 Laclede, office secretary at Procter & Gamble

William M. & Amalie Presley, 341 Laclede, clerk

Willie Presley, 115 South Parkway West, employee at AM Finishing

612 Scotty Moore, Jr. married Mary Durkee on March 12, 1950.

613 Elvis started dating at the age of fifteen.

614 Joseph Beaulieu legally adopted Priscilla on April 17, 1950.

615 In 1950, James Tipler, who later went on to own Crown Electric, was an electrician at the Townsend Electric Co. Born on December 26, 1921, James lived at 1850 Felix Avenue.

616 Elvis frequented Porky's Drive-In located at 848 Thomas. Porky's Drive-In was owned by Marvin Hardy, who lived at 856 S. Greer. Ruby Beasley was a helper at Porky's. She lived at 947 Worner.

617 In 1950, Bill (William) Black and his wife, Evelyn, lived at 1317 Oak Street in Memphis. Bill was a mechanic at the time. Mrs. Ruby Black, his mother, lived at 1052 Beach.

618 While in high school, Elvis occasionally saved his money so that he could have his hair styled in a beauty parlor.

619 In the early 1950's, Elvis sometimes used Rose Oil Hair Tonic.

620 It was reported that Elvis earned a "C" in both his music class and his shop class at L.C. Humes High School in the 1949-1950 school year.

621 Elvis was absent for 10 days during the 1949-1950 school year.

622 The Korean War was in full swing when Elvis was in high school. It began in June of 1950 and lasted until July of 1953.

623 Sam Phillips promoted bands at the Peabody Hotel in the spring of 1950.

624 Sam Phillips' first job at a record company was with Modern Records in Los Angeles, California, in early June of 1950. He cut custom tape sessions with jazz pianist Phineas Newton. It was shortly after this job that Sam opened his own recording studio.

Elvis photographed while changing a tire as part of the Memphis Road-E-O contest in October of 1952. As winner of the contest, Elvis was named Mr. Safety.

625   Sam Phillips was a studio engineer living at 1928 Vinton Avenue with his wife Betsy when he opened the Memphis Recording Service in 1950. The studio was located at 706 Union Avenue and the telephone number there was 527-7197.

626   Sam Phillips' partner in the Memphis Recording Service was Jim Bulleit (b. November 4, 1908). Jim put up half the money to open the studio.

627   Sam Phillips paid $150 a month in rent for the Union Avenue building which housed the Memphis Recording Service. The building was originally a car radiator shop called Automobile Row.

628   Sam Phillips and his secretary, Marion Keisker, remodeled the interior of the Memphis Recording Service studio themselves. They installed acoustic tiles on the walls and ceiling.

629   Sam Phillips' Memphis Recording Service recorded any and all events, including weddings, bar mitzvahs, and christenings, onto one-sided, single-faced LPs. The cost for this service was $9.

630   In 1950, Dewey Phillips was a salesman for W.T. Grant Co. and lived at 1041 Walker Avenue in Memphis.

631   In 1950, Delbert "Sonny" West worked as a doorman. He lived at 644 Somerville Mall, Apt. H, in Memphis.

632   In 1950, an Elvis Tanser was living in Memphis at 615 Polk Avenue. He worked as a waiter.

633   In 1950, Alberta Holman and her husband, Odis, lived at 2281 Zanone Avenue in Memphis. She would become Elvis's maid at Graceland.

634 In 1950, the mayor of Memphis was S. Watkins Overton, for whom the Overton Park Shell was named a few years later.

635 The First Assembly of God Church pastor in 1950 was Reverend James E. Hamill (b. April 15, 1913). The church was located at 960 S. 3rd Street in Memphis.

636 In 1950, the Memphian Theater's manager was Joseph Keifer. The theater was located at 51 S. Cooper. Elvis began attending the theater in the 1950's and later rented it for private screenings with friends in the 1960's and 1970's.

637 During the early to late 1950's, Elvis ate Italian food at a restaurant called Sam's Spaghetti House located at 73 Poplar Ave. The restaurant was owned by Samuel J. and Rose Sciara, who resided at 845 N. Trezevant. Employees of Sam's Spaghetti House included assistant manager O.A. Robinson, waiters Eddie Neeley and Robert L. Walter, and cook Mary Parson.

638 MALCO Theaters Inc. was run by president Maurice A. Lightman, who lived at 197 S. Main Street. This was another theater that Elvis attended and later rented a few times.

639 The owner of the Hi-Hat Cafe was Clifton Graves, who resided at 1675 Madison Avenue. One of the waitresses at the Hi-Hat Cafe was Juanita Burfield, who lived at 660 Firestone Ct. Elvis enjoyed going there with friends because the Hi-Hat had live entertainment.

640 The Curtain Shop at 150 Madison in Memphis was owned by Edward C. Locke. It was reported that Gladys worked there for a very short time.

641 In the early to mid-1950's, Elvis played football with black kids from his neighborhood in Memphis at the Parkway Pumping Station, located at 488 N. Dunlap.

642 The Strand Theater, where Elvis went to watch the latest movies, was located at 138 S. Main St. in Memphis. In 1950, the general manager of the theater was Jack Katz, who lived at 18 N. Highland. Three of the projectionists at the Strand Theater were Robert de Graffenreid (909 Garland), James A. Grooms (1992 Union Ave.), and A.J. Suzore (1590 Jackson Ave.). One of the ushers at the Strand was Arthur Hazlett (67 W. Mallory Ave.), and the maid was Laura Campbell (395 Pontontoc).

643 There was another "Elvis" living in Memphis in the 1950s; Elvis L. Rubin lived at 2476 Union Avenue.

644 Edwin G. Fitzpatrick was the department manager at O.K. Houck Piano Co., where Elvis hocked one of his guitars. Fitzpatrick's home address was 878 1/2 Decatur. Vera Thornberry was a clerk at the company and resided at 1572 Overton Park, Apt. H.

645 Edward H. Crump (b. May 8, 1903) was the president of the E.H. Crump & Co. Bank, and E.H. Crump Stadium, located on Linden Avenue at Cleveland Street, was named for him. Elvis enjoyed watching football games there and, in the middle to late 1950's, he frequented the stadium, which was the largest in Memphis, seating 20,000.

646 The Southern Bowling Lanes Inc. were located at 299 N. Cleveland in Memphis. The owners and officers were Aaron Brenner (president), George T. Perkins (vice president), and Joseph H. Altfater (secretary/treasurer). Elvis had a confrontation with a hustler there and broke a cue stick.

647   Elvis's tenth grade homeroom teacher at L.C. Humes High School was Ms. Williams.

648   Elvis was absent from school for 13 days during the 1950-1951 school year.

649   Elvis received two "F's" in typing class during his sophomore year at L.C. Humes High School.

650   The superintendent of Memphis City Schools while Elvis was a student was E.C. Ball.

651   From 1949 to 1953, the L.C. Humes High School cafeteria manager was Mrs. Lucille Garrison.

652   While in high school, Elvis enjoyed history, English, and government.

653   The Presleys owned a parakeet that they kept in a wooden cage which Elvis had made in shop class.

654   Knowing how poor the Presleys were, Elvis's shop teacher at L.C. Humes High School often brought lunch for Elvis.

655   Gladys walked Elvis to school every day until he was 15 years old.

656   In high school, Elvis was mocked by his peers. He was called "Gorgeous George" because he was the only boy at school to dress up and to always comb his hair.

657   Elvis sometimes invited friends home from school, where he would sing to them in the basement.

658 On September 4, 1950, Elvis surprised his L.C. Humes High School classmate Doris Guy Wallace by singing at her 14th birthday party.

659 One of Elvis's classmates at L.C. Humes High School was W. Kenneth Holdwitch. He became a professor.

660 Elvis kept (and autographed!) the first dollar he earned from his first paycheck.

661 As a teenager, Elvis wanted a 1932 roadster or a Ford Model T. If he'd had a choice, however, he would have preferred the roadster.

662 Gladys Presley was a coffee server at Britling's Cafeteria in 1950. She was also responsible for filling and cleaning the coffee urns. The Cafeteria was located next to Loew's State Theater in Memphis.

663 As a teen, Elvis considered his father to be a lazy person and had little respect for him. Elvis had to force himself to show respect for Vernon in public.

664 In the 1950's, Elvis worked bagging and delivering groceries at Babe Wade's Red White Store located on Alabama Street in Memphis.

665 As a teen, Elvis wanted to work as a gas station attendant.

666 Elvis tried to grow a mustache as a teenager, but because his hair was so blonde, no one could see it.

667 The three most popular night clubs in Memphis during Elvis's teen years were The Plantation Inn, The Cotton Club Cafe, and Danny's Cafe, all located in West Memphis. Danny's Cafe was located at 160 Court Avenue and was owned by Daniel Trabish. The Cotton Club

A 17-year-old Elvis on the front steps of the Lauderdale Courts in the summer of 1952.

Cafe was located at 75 McCall Place and was owned by Mildred Hall.

668   The hot spots of Beale Street during the 1940's and 1950's were The Monarch Hippodrome, Pee Wee's Saloon, Panama Club, Casino Henry, and Ruben Cherry's Home of the Blues. Elvis visited each of these establishments at one time or another.

669   A teenage Elvis and his friends visited the Green Beetle Club, located at 325 S. Main, one block from Beale Street in downtown Memphis. The owner of the Green Beetle was Frank Liberto. The cafe's cashier was Ann P. Beverly, who lived at 2112 S. Parkway E., and the cook was Lillie Blue, who resided at 366 Hernando.

670   Elvis began suffering from insomnia in the early 1950's.

671   In the 1950's, Colonel Tom Parker owned a house in Madison, Tennessee, that had once belonged to Eddy Arnold. It is reported that the Colonel conned Arnold into giving the house to him.

672   On December 16, 1950, Linda Moore was born to Scotty and Mary Moore.

673   Scotty Moore was reportedly a dry cleaner and hat specialist just before launching his career as a working musician.

674   Elvis's uncle, Vester Presley, dreamed of becoming a country and western star.

675   Gladys Presley sang and played the harmonica quite well.

676   Elvis had a bad habit of biting his nails.

677 Elvis received his driver's license in January 1951, when he turned 16. He used his Uncle Travis's car to take the exam in Memphis.

678 Vernon bought Elvis a 1942 Lincoln Zephyr for $50 in 1951. Elvis was thrilled to own his first car. He and his father cleaned, washed, and waxed it almost every day.

679 Elvis drove his car to school every day. Reportedly, he was one of only two students at L.C. Humes High School who owned their own cars.

680 The school day at L.C. Humes High School ended at 2:15 p.m.

681 Luther Nall was one of Elvis's good friends at L.C. Humes High School. After high school, Luther worked in aviation.

682 While in high school, Elvis dreamed of becoming a professional football player. Elvis tried out for the L.C. Humes High School football team, the Tigers, but without success. The coach of the Tigers in 1951 was Lee Thompson.

683 Elvis played in some of the football scrimmage games at L.C. Humes High School in the summer of 1951, but his mother forced him to quit because she was afraid he would get hurt.

684 Elvis performed a duet at L.C. Humes High School with his friend, James Gault. Elvis played the guitar and James played the accordion.

685 Elvis joined the L.C. Humes High School ROTC (Reserve Officers Training Camp) as a sophomore in 1951. He was in the A Company, second platoon.

686 Elvis's ROTC sergeant at L.C. Humes High School was Robert

McIntyre (b. August 3, 1923) and his platoon captain was Charley Fisher.

687   Red West, who was a year behind Elvis in school, was also in the L.C. Humes High School ROTC. He also served in the A Company, second platoon.

688   During high school, Red West lived in a housing project called Hurt Village.

689   The L.C. Humes High School creed was, "This new day I dedicate myself under God, to the opportunities before me. I consecrate my mind to development, my hands to usefulness, as I strive for a better world for those who will come after me even as I benefit today from the efforts of those who had gone before me. This is my creed and my task."

690   Elvis made his mother a cutting board and a salad bowl in shop class, both of which Gladys treasured.

691   In 1951, during his sophomore year at L.C. Humes High School, Elvis failed all of his exams except shop.

692   One of Elvis's good female friends at L.C. Humes High School was Katie Mae Shook.

693   Elvis was absent a total of 24 days during the 1951-1952 school year.

694   Dewey Phillips ran "Red, Hot & Blue," the hottest show on the air, on WHBQ Radio in Memphis. Elvis listened to Dewey's show, which played current R&B and rockabilly hits, every day. Dewey's radio nickname was "Daddy-O" Dewey.

695   WHBQ Radio's major sponsor was Falstaff Beer. Dewey Phillips was the station's most popular DJ.

696   In 1951, Dewey Phillips was involved in a car accident. As a result, he was partially crippled.

697   Vernon bought Elvis an $8 record player from Sears & Roebuck in 1951. The first albums Elvis played on his phonograph were 78 rpms, not 45's.

698   Elvis's uncle, Vester Presley, once worked in a Memphis bakery.

699   Corrine Tate was one of Elvis's cousins.

700   Harold Loyd, Elvis's cousin, married a woman named Marcella sometime in the 1950's. The couple had a son, David, soon thereafter.

701   At 5'11", Minnie Mae Presley was almost as tall as Elvis.

702   Minnie Mae Presley, Elvis's grandmother, would not allow anyone to kiss her on the mouth, as she thought it was very unsanitary.

703   Brenda Smith, one of Elvis's cousins, was born in 1951.

704   In the 1950's, Elvis loved to listen to WDIA Radio, a popular R&B station. With the power of 50,000 watts, it reached a market of 1,237,700, or 10% of America's black population. The station was owned by Bert Ferguson and John R. Pepper and was broadcast from 2074 Union Ave. The telephone number was 36-2703.

705   WDIA Radio announcers in the 1950's were Ed Cade, who lived at 276 Garland, and Ed Daniels, who lived at 3542 Barbara Circle.

706   In the 1950's, WMPS Radio was broadcast from 112 Union Avenue. The vice president/general manager was Harold R. Krelstein, and the station's telephone number was 5-2721. The station's two engineers were James Dearing, who lived at 1215 Knox Road, and Ray Dickson, who resided at 172 Kimbrough Place, Apt. 501. One of the announcers was Albert A. Bensabut Jr., who lived at 2246 South Parkway E., Apt. 18. WMPS was one of Elvis's favorites and also was one of the first to play Elvis's music.

707   In the 1950's, WHBQ Radio was broadcast from the Hotel Gayoso at 139 S. Main Street. The station's general manager was John H. Cleghorn, and the telephone number was 8-6868. The engineer at WHBQ Radio was Robert Harbison, who lived at 900 N. Holmes. One of the announcers was William Gordon, who lived at 3712 Kenwood Ave. WHBQ was another of Elvis's favorites in Memphis, and they too played Elvis in the early years.

708   In the 1950's, WHHM Radio was broadcast out of the 433 Sterick Building and the general manager was Patt McDonald. The WHHM transmitter was located at 46 Neely. One of their announcers was Ronnie Evans, who lived at 1420 Cameron. This was another popular station in Memphis, and one Elvis liked to listen to as well.

709   The Singer Sewing Machine Company headquarters were located in Memphis at 84 N. Main. The manager was George E. Murray. In the 1950's, the company's phone numbers were 5-1797 and 8-5143. Another branch of the company was located at 3405 Summer Avenue, and was managed by Lewis E. Keith. This company sponsored Elvis's Comeback Special in 1968.

710   On June 3, 1951, Elvis, with the help of his uncle Johnny, got a job with the Precision Tool Company in Memphis.

Elvis with his two best friends, Buzzy Forbes and Farley Guy, at the Lauderdale Courts in 1952.

711 The Precision Tool Company, which manufactured ammunition, was located at 3116 E. Mallory Ave. The president of the company was Hugh D. Barkett Jr., the vice president was Harry E. O'Harra, and the secretary was Billy Stafford.

712 Working from 7:00 a.m. to 3:30 p.m., Elvis earned $30 a week from the Precision Tool Company. His badge number was 78. Vernon and Vester Presley both worked at the Precision Tool Company at the same time Elvis did.

713 On July 1, 1951, Elvis was fired from the Precision Tool Company for being under age. Elvis was only sixteen years old.

714 Ed Parker, who became Elvis's Kempo instructor and good friend, served in the Coast Guard during the Korean War.

715 Elvis sang in the East Trigg M.B. Church's choir while in high school. The church was located at 1189 Trigg Avenue in Memphis. Sunday school services were held at 9:30 and 11:00 a.m. The pastor of the church was W. Herbert Brewster.

716 At 16 years of age, Elvis let his crewcut grow out and attempted to grow sideburns. By late fall of 1951, Elvis was sporting a ducktail and sideburns.

717 It was rumored that, as a teenager, Elvis sneaked into black neighborhoods looking to have sex with black girls.

718 In the early 1950's, a men's clothing store located down the street from Lansky's had on display the tuxedo Machine Gun Kelly was wearing when he was killed. When Elvis saw the bullet-riddled suit, he found it disgusting.

719 Scotty Moore, Jr. was discharged from the U.S. Navy on January 4, 1952.

720 Sam Phillips started Sun Studios in February of 1952.

721 The Sun Studios logo, a rooster set against a sun, was designed by a commercial artist from Beale Street in 1952.

722 Shortly after starting Sun Records, Sam Phillips was sued by the Sun-Ray Company from Albuquerque, New Mexico for use of the name Sun. Sam won!

723 The Sun Records warehouse was operated by Sam Phillips's older brother, Thomas. He took care of inventory, shipping, and returns.

724 On March 27, 1952, the first Sun records were pressed.

725 The 45 and 78 rpm records first produced by Sun Records in the 1950's were pressed by companies such as Plastic Products, located at 1746 Chelsea Avenue in Memphis. Their phone number was 35-7160.

726 Elvis's favorite colors in the early 1950's were pink and black.

727 Elvis bought his first "hip" outfit at Nate Epstein's Pawn Shop, located at 162-66 Beale Street in Memphis. Their motto was "We loan on articles of value." It was after this purchase that Elvis started to dress in what the white population of the time referred to as the "Negro style." Store owner Nathan Epstein and his wife, Pearl, lived at 661 East Drive.

728 Elvis hated to wear shorts because he thought his legs were too skinny.

729 Elvis saw movies at the Suzore #2 Theater located at 279 North Main Street in Memphis in the early 1950's. In 1952 and 1953, admission to the theater was 15¢. The theater was owned by Fred J. Suzore.

730 Fred Suzore's wife Irene ran the Suzore #1 Theater at 869 Jackson in Memphis. The couple lived at 867 Jackson. It was reported that Elvis ran to this theater when his song first played on the radio; this information is inaccurate, as Elvis was at home when he first heard his song.

731 In the 1950's, Elvis's favorite movies were comedies and westerns.

732 In the 1950's, Elvis was quoted as saying that his mother's bacon and eggs was his favorite meal.

733 After school, Gladys sometimes made Elvis his favorite peanut butter and banana sandwiches. She sat with him while he ate and they discussed how their days had been.

734 In mid-April of 1952, Elvis worked as an usher at Loew's State Theater. Located at 152 South Main Street and next door to Mullins and Wells Credit, the theater was just five blocks from Elvis's house in Memphis.

735 When working at Loew's State Theater in Memphis, Elvis's uniform consisted of a brown jacket, tan pants with brown stripes on the sides, and a white shirt.

736 To work at Loew's State Theater, Elvis needed a Social Security card. Elvis's Social Security number was 409-52-2002.

737 Elvis worked from 5:00 to 10:00 p.m., five days a week at Loew's

State Theater in Memphis. At 50¢ an hour, he earned $12.50 a week.

738 After work at Loew's State Theater, Elvis met his friends at an all-night diner called the Grit-Iron, later known as the Gridiron. The Gridiron System, Inc., chain was owned by Harris Scheuner and had 11 locations throughout Memphis in 1950. They were located at 1142 Union Avenue, 2318 Lamar Avenue, 438 N. Cleveland, 898 Madison Avenue, 711 S. Dudley, 1811 Madison Avenue, 1102 Lamar Avenue, 266 E. McLemore Avenue, 1693 Lamar Avenue, 1359 Poplar Avenue, and 22 N. 3rd (the one Elvis most likely visited while working at Loew's Theater).

739 During the time that he worked at Loew's State Theater, Elvis earned money on weekends by mowing lawns for 50¢ per lawn.

740 While Elvis worked at Loew's State Theater in Memphis, his mother worked next door at Britling's Cafeteria.

741 Britling's Cafeteria had three locations: 75 Union Avenue (where Gladys Presley worked), telephone number 37-8644; 155 Madison Avenue, telephone number 5-3191; and 157 Madison Avenue, telephone number 5-8577.

742 The president of the Britling's Cafeteria Company of Tennessee, Gladys Presley's employer, was Boswell A.W. Johnson, who lived at 2291 Jefferson Avenue. The vice president was L.E. Johnson. The secretary/treasurer was Glenn G. Davidson.

743 Arthur H. Groom was the manager at the Loew's State Theater. He lived at 3175 Jackson Avenue. On May 28, 1952, Mr. Groom fired Elvis from his job after Elvis got into a fight with a co-worker.

744 Co-workers of Gladys Presley when she worked at Britling's Cafeteria were Glenn G. Davidson, the general house manager, and Joseph A. Enochs, the manager of the restaurant.

745 Before Elvis discovered Lansky's, he bought his clothes from the Federal Credit Clothing Store, owned by Herbert A. Tucker, located at 174 S. Main Street in Memphis.

746 In 1950, Lansky Bros. Uniform Company was located at 126 Beale Street with another branch at 244 N. Main Street in Memphis. Their phone numbers were 5-5401 and 37-0116 respectively.

747 The advertising slogan for Lansky Bros. Uniform Company was "Tailor-made uniforms for men and women. We have all types of emblems and lettering."

748 There were five Lansky brothers who owned the Lansky Bros. Uniform Company: Frank Lansky (890 N. Watkins), Guy G. Lansky (890 N. Watkins), Irvin Lansky (502 N. Claybrook), Alvin Lansky (890 N. Watkins), and Bernard J. Lansky (1349 Jackson Ave).

749 Next door to the Lansky Bros. Uniform Co. on Beale Street was the Boston Dry Goods Store, located at #125. Other businesses situated next to Lansky's were Max Siegel Shoe Repair (#127), The Blue Light Studio (#130), and Nathan Novick Men's Clothing (#131).

750 Lansky's Clothing Emporium, as it was later called, was the only clothing store in Memphis willing to give Elvis Presley store credit.

751 The payment plan agreed upon by Elvis and the Lansky brothers to pay off his credit bill at Lansky's Clothing Emporium was "a dollar down and a dollar every week."

Elvis standing in front of his 1939 Lincoln Zephyr, 1953.

752   Elvis paid off his first credit bill at Lansky's with his first paycheck from Loew's State Theater.

753   In 1952, Bob Neal opened a record store at 505 Main Street in Memphis, next door to the Warner Theater.

754   By 1952, Bob Neal had founded the popular Memphis Promotions Agency.

755   On August 6, 1952, Elvis began work at the Upholsteries Specialties Company, located at 210 W. Georgia Avenue in Memphis. They did a lot of work for Elvis in later years.

756   Marty Lacker attended Central High School in 1952, and later transferred to L.C. Humes High School. According to Marty, he met Elvis in 1952.

757   Red West rescued Elvis from a haircut courtesy of school bullies one day in the bathroom at L.C. Humes High School. Red was known as a tough guy, and he bullied the bad guys into letting Elvis go.

758   Elvis's weight was between 160 and 185 pounds during his high school years.

759   Walter Doxey (b. August 22, 1914) was the L.C. Humes High School boxing coach when Elvis attended the school.

760   In 1952, Elvis's eleventh grade homeroom teacher at L.C. Humes High School was Mrs. Virginia Lee Alexander, whose home was at 1667 Lawrence Place.

761   The L.C. Humes High School treasurer for the 1952-1953 school year

was Mrs. T.C. (Lucille) Young. She lived at 684 Decatur in Memphis.

762 The L.C. Humes High School historian for the 1952-1953 school year was Mrs. Henry L. (Christine) Schneider. She lived at 3032 Old Benjestown Road in Memphis.

763 Elvis took several electronics classes in high school with the hope of becoming an electrician.

764 In September of 1952, Elvis got a job at the MARL Metal Manufacturing Company, located at 208 Georgia Avenue in Memphis. Robert Bozoff hired Elvis.

765 MARL Metal Manufacturing Company owners were president Louis Bozoff (777 Hollywood; wife, Anne); vice president Nathan Bozoff (703 S. Highland; wife, Quay); secretary Albert Bozoff (641 E. McLemore Ave; wife, Mildred); and treasurer Robert Bozoff (3835 Chicadee Ave; wife, Alma).

766 The office secretary at MARL Metal Mfg. Co. was Dorthea Paswater, who lived at 1279 Carrolton Rd. Hazel L. Washington was a painter for the company and resided at 1058 N. Claybrook.

767 Elvis made $1 an hour working at MARL. He worked in the fabrication division, making plastic table tops for the MARL dinettes line. Elvis, along with two other employees, worked the late shift from 3:15 p.m. until midnight. Elvis's job included sweeping the floor of metal scraps, debris, and paper.

768 Elvis worked at MARL Metal Company for just two months. When Gladys found out that her son had been falling asleep at school, she forced him to quit the job in November of 1952.

769 Mildred Scrivener (b. January 22, 1892) was Elvis's senior year homeroom and history teacher at L.C. Humes High School.

770 Fred Frederick met Elvis in shop class at L.C. Humes High School. He became a policeman.

771 Elvis enjoyed shop class at L.C. Humes High School. His teacher stated that Elvis's crafts turned out exceptionally well.

772 George Klein was president of the senior class at L.C. Humes High School in 1952-1953. He majored in science, math, and English, and received "Best Platoon" and "Best Company" awards from the ROTC.

773 In October of 1952, Elvis was named "Mr. Safety" by the Memphis Road-E-O Contest sponsored by the Junior Chamber of Commerce. A photo of Elvis changing a tire appeared in the local newspaper.

774 Red West participated in the following clubs while attending L.C. Humes High School: the Key Club, the Hi-Y Club, the Optimist Club, and the "H" Club.

775 Red West was Miss Flois Gwaltney's library assistant at L.C. Humes High School.

776 Tammy Young was one of Elvis's high school friends. They enjoyed playing pool together.

777 Elvis reportedly kept a phonograph in his locker at school and played his favorite records during lunch.

778 Mrs. Engle W. (Eva) Nelius was the advisory vice president during

After graduating from high school, Elvis worked for the Crown Electric Company. Here co-owner Gladys Tipler looks at Elvis's name, which he carved into a wall while employed there.

the 1952-1953 school year at L.C. Humes High School. She lived at 772 N. Dunlap in Memphis.

779 Mrs. Richard R. (Virginia) Spore was the first vice president and aide to the principal during the 1952-1953 school year at Elvis's L.C. Humes High School. She lived at 1143 Decatur in Memphis.

780 When Elvis was a senior at L.C. Humes High School, his fifth period class was English. He sat in the last seat of the second row nearest the door.

781 Elvis's biology teacher at L.C. Humes High School was Miss Schilling. He sat in the back of her classroom, in the last seat of the second row nearest the window.

782 In 1952, Dr. William Robert Hunt, the doctor who delivered Elvis, died in Tupelo, Mississippi, at the age of 85.

783 Elvis and his friends enjoyed going to parties, going to the movies, sitting on the steps of the Lauderdale Courts and talking, looking at girls, and playing football.

784 Tom Parker innovated the independent booking agency, which became the "in" thing.

785 Tom Parker relied on Tampa, Florida, printer Clyde Realsi to create promotional materials for the Humane Society, Eddy Arnold, and eventually Elvis.

786 Gladys Presley's favorite beverage was beer.

787 In late 1952, Elvis reportedly sold a pint of blood to Baptist Memorial Hospital for $10.

788   Elvis never dotted the letter "i" when he wrote.

789   On December 12, 1952, Donald Moore was born to Scotty and Mary Moore.

790   After the birth of his son, Scotty Moore filed for divorce.

791   Elvis hosted a New Year's Eve party for his friends at the Lauderdale Courts in 1952.

792   Elvis attended dances at St. Mary's Church on a regular basis. The church was located at 155 Market Street and the pastor was Rev. Wilfred Cool.

793   In late 1952, Mrs. Jane Richardson of the Memphis Housing Authority made the decision to evict the Presleys from their Lauderdale Courts home because they were making too much money to qualify for assistance.

794   The Presleys were evicted from the Lauderdale Courts on January 7, 1953.

795   The Presleys immediately moved to an apartment at 698 Saffarans Street after being evicted from the Lauderdale Courts. The 2-room apartment rented for $10 a month and was located directly behind L.C. Humes High School. The Presleys lived there until April of 1953.

796   Prior to Elvis and his parents moving into the 698 Saffarans house in Memphis, James H. Petty and his wife Elizabeth lived there.

797   Despite what many authors have reported, the Presleys never lived at 398 Cypress Street.

798 William Job Stanley, Jr. was born on January 18, 1953. In 1960, when his mother married Elvis's father, he became Elvis's step-brother. It has been reported that William Stanley, Jr. was born in Japan; in fact, he was born in Fort Monroe, Virginia.

799 Elvis and his friend, Buzzy Forbes, liked to go to the Green Owl, a beer bar located at 260 N. Main Street in Memphis. Considered a "club for black people," the Green Owl played only R&B music.

800 In the 1950's, Elvis enjoyed sneaking into the Hotel Men's Improvement Club, a local blues club, to "watch the black people perform."

801 In February of 1953, Elvis went to Blake's Coiffure Shop to get a trim. Blake Johnson, the owner, cut a bit more off than Elvis wanted. Elvis got angry and left in a huff.

802 In April of 1953, the Presleys moved from their Saffarans Street apartment to 462 Alabama Street in Memphis. Their new landlady was Mrs. Millie Dubrovner.

803 The Presleys paid $50 a month in rent for the downstairs apartment of a two-story brick house on Alabama Street in Memphis. Vernon and Gladys shared the only bedroom. Elvis slept on the couch in the living room and his grandmother, Minnie Mae, slept on a cot in the dining room.

804 The Presleys' telephone number at their Alabama Street apartment in Memphis was 37-4185. They lived there until late 1954.

805 Alfred and Jeanette Fruchter lived above the Presleys on Alabama Street in Memphis. Alfred was a rabbi at the Beth El-Emeth

Synagogue. The Fruchters' home phone number was 37-5630. They were good friends of the Presleys.

806   When the Presleys could not afford to pay their water bill (which was often), their Alabama Street neighbor, Jeanette Fruchter, paid it for them.

807   TV Guide was founded in 1953 by Walter Annenberg. Elvis appeared on the cover nine times.

808   Some time in 1953, Elvis borrowed a book from the L.C. Humes High School library entitled *Second Book of Marvels—The Orient*. He had the book checked out for seven days.

809   At 8:00 p.m. on Thursday, April 9, 1953, Elvis participated in the L.C. Humes High School Band Annual Minstrel as the guitarist. In the program for the event, his name is misspelled as "Prestly."

810   Elvis wore a red plaid shirt borrowed from his friend, Buzzy Forbes, for the L.C. Humes High School Band Annual Minstrel in 1953. He sang "Cold, Cold Icy Fingers." After receiving the loudest applause from the 1,500 people in attendance, he performed an encore, singing "Till I Waltz Again With You."

811   In 1953, Tom Parker was the publicity man for Frank Goad Clement, who was running for Governor of Tennessee. Clement won and, to thank Parker, bestowed the honorary title of "Colonel" upon him.

812   Thomas Diskin became Colonel Tom Parker's assistant in 1953. Diskin, who was Parker's brother-in-law, was working for Jamboree Attractions in Chicago just before accepting his new position. Diskin, who was from Chicago, had a background in accounting. He later helped the Colonel with Elvis's career.

813   Eddy Arnold fired Colonel Parker as his manager in 1953.

814   In 1953, Scotty Moore had a relationship with Francis Tucker which resulted in the birth of a daughter, Victoria.

815   Scotty Moore traded his guitar for a Gibson ES 295, a cello-shaped, semi-acoustic jazz model, in the spring of 1953. This is the guitar he used when recording with Elvis at Sun Studios.

816   For a short time in early 1953, Elvis worked at Farmer's Market in Memphis as a truck driver.

817   As a teenager, Elvis had a severe acne problem, which resulted in some minor facial scarring. In addition to his face, the acne also affected his back.

818   Elvis had three warts on his right hand. He had a double wart on his wrist and another on the knuckle of his forefinger.

819   Elvis detested blue jeans, as they were the only thing he wore during his school days. After his rise to fame, he swore he would never wear them again, and he rarely did.

820   Elvis enjoyed playing football with his friends from the neighborhood at the Parkway Pumping Station, also known as the "Water Works," located at North Parkway and Dunlap Street in Memphis.

821   Elvis began smoking cigars in 1953. He tried to hide this as much as he could; after he became famous, he would not allow photographs to be taken of him while he was enjoying a cigar.

822   Gene Smith, Elvis's cousin, worked at Hall's Grocery at 1588

Sam Phillips, owner of Sun Studios.

Mississippi Blvd. in Memphis in the early to mid-1950's. He delivered groceries on a bicycle.

823 Carroll "Junior" Smith, Elvis's cousin, served in the 38th Infantry during the Korean War.

824 On May 24, 1953, Elvis entered a contest at The Jimmie Rodger's Father of Country Music Festival at the Lamar Hotel in Meridian, Mississippi. He won a guitar.

825 Elvis's senior prom was held at the famous Peabody Hotel in downtown Memphis. The hotel was located at 149 Union Avenue and, at the time, the phone number was 8-7766. The president and vice president of the hotel were Frank R. Schutt and W.P. Holliday, respectively.

826 Elvis's prom suit came from Lansky's Clothing Emporium. He was the only student to wear a pink tuxedo, a black shirt and bow tie, and a pink and black cummerbund.

827 It has been reported that Elvis lost his virginity right around the time he graduated from L.C. Humes High School in 1953.

828 Elvis's report cards from L.C. Humes High School listed his home addresses as 370 Washington, 185 Winchester, and 462 Alabama.

829 Elvis received an "F" in shop class at the end of his senior year.

830 Elvis was absent a total of 28 days during the 1952-1953 school year.

831 In the 1953 edition of the L.C. Humes High School yearbook, *The Herald*, the caption near Elvis's picture read: Presley, Elvis Aron. Major: Shop, History, English. Activities: ROTC, Biology Club,

English Club, History Club, Speech Club.

832 Elvis's senior yearbook photo was positioned between Robert Earl Perry's and Shirley Ruleman's.

833 On June 2, 1953, L.C. Humes High School had a picnic at Maywood Beach for graduating seniors. Elvis wore a black shirt with white trim, jeans, and light colored moccasins to the event.

834 Elvis spent some time at his senior class picnic with classmate Rosemary Barraco.

835 On June 3, 1953, Elvis graduated as part of L.C. Humes High School's 202nd class, along with 200 other students.

836 The L.C. Humes High School Class of 1953 graduation ceremony took place at the Ellis Auditorium, located at 225 North Main Street in Memphis.

837 Ernest C. Ball (b. August 8, 1895) presented a graduating Elvis with his high school diploma in 1953.

838 The 1953 L.C. Humes High School president was Milton Bowers (b. February 15, 1898), secretary was O.H. James, superintendent was Ernest C. Ball, and principal was Thomas C. Brindley.

839 William Leaptrott was a friend of Elvis's who also graduated from L.C. Humes High School in 1953.

840 Marie Henson Pittman went to L.C. Humes High School with Elvis and graduated the same year.

841   Shelby County Deputy Bill Morris's wife graduated with Elvis from L.C. Humes High School in June of 1953.

842   Elvis weighed 185 pounds when he graduated from high school.

843   Jeanette and Alfred Fruchter, the Presley's neighbors, presented Elvis with his first set of cufflinks as a graduation gift. Elvis wore the set, which cost $2, to the graduation ceremony.

844   When Elvis graduated from high school in 1953, the President of the United States was Dwight D. Eisenhower.

845   Several hours after graduation, Elvis took the general aptitude test battery at the Tennessee Employment Security office located at 122 Union in Memphis. Mrs. Weir Harris administered the test. Elvis's scores were average in all subjects except manual dexterity. As those scores were less than average, test administrators felt it might be difficult to find a job for him.

846   A short time after taking the general aptitude test battery on the day of his high school graduation, Elvis was notified about a job opportunity at M.B. Parker's Machine Shop.

847   M.B. Parker Co., Inc., where Elvis worked for a short while, was located at 1449 Thomas and the phone numbers there were 5-8102 and 8-4673. The company was owned by Malcolm B. Parker and his wife, Ruth, who lived at 748 Charles Place in Memphis. They advertised themselves as "Manufacturers Complete Machine Shop—Sheet Metal Welding Facilities & Founders of Gray Iron, Brass and Aluminum Casting."

848   Some of the employees at the M.B. Parker Company when Elvis

worked there were accountant Lawrence W. Wineman, who lived at 905 N. Idlewild; secretary Gus Ferguson; Eddie E. Taylor; Elmor Taylor; and Joseph D. Wray.

849   Elvis's job at M.B. Parker's Machine Shop was to pry old nail heads off flame-thrower regulators from the depot, replace them with O-rings, put the heads back on, load them, and take them back to the depot.

850   Elvis worked at M.B. Parker's Machine Shop from early June of 1953 until September of that year. Pay day was on Saturday.

851   Scotty Moore married for the second time in June of 1953. His bride was Bobbie Walls. The couple was married in Mississippi.

852   In July of 1953, Elvis got a job at the Crown Electric Company owned by James Tipler and his wife, Gladys (b. August 12, 1919). Located at 353 Poplar Avenue in Memphis, the company's phone number was 5-4625.

853   When Elvis first started working at Crown Electric, his job was that of stock boy. He was later promoted to a delivery position. The youngest employee at the company, he was paid $1.25 an hour.

854   For a short time, Elvis drove a black 1950 Chevrolet pickup truck for Crown Electric.

855   After working at Crown Electric for a while, Elvis had the added responsibility of pulling wire and stacking pipes.

856   While working at Crown Electric during the day, Elvis was also going to night school to be an electrician. Certified electricians earned $3 an hour at the time.

857   The $35 paycheck Elvis earned each week from Crown Electric was handed over to his mother on Saturday nights.

858   On several of Elvis's paychecks in mid-July of 1953, his first name was misspelled "Alvis."

859   Crown Electric had a bank account with the Crosstown branch of the First National Bank of Memphis.

860   Mr. and Mrs. Tipler, owners of Crown Electric, took Elvis to a local beauty parlor one day and forced him to get a haircut.

861   Shortly after Elvis started working at Crown Electric, he needed a truck of his own. He was turned down for a loan by every bank in Memphis except one: The National Bank of Commerce, located at 45 S. Second Street.

862   Jack D. Stovall (b. December 28, 1904) was vice president of the National Bank of Commerce in Memphis. He and his wife, Miriam, lived at 3181 Carnes Ave. Mr. Stovall was the only person to give Elvis bank credit when he was working for Crown Electric.

863   After receiving the loan from The National Bank of Commerce and purchasing a Ford F-100 pickup truck in 1953, Elvis maintained his relationship with this bank for the rest of his life.

864   While Elvis was working at Crown Electric in Memphis, his cousin, Gene Smith, worked as a soda jerk in a local drugstore.

865   Bill Black worked for Firestone Stores in Memphis when Elvis was at Crown Electric. They had three locations: 1030 Linden Ave., telephone # 2-3181, managed by J. Howard Swaim; 1694 Jackson

Marion Keisker, Sam Phillips's secretary and assistant at Sun Studios. She became the first to discover Elvis when he entered the Memphis Recording Service on July 18, 1953.

Ave., telephone # 7-2876; and 156 N. 3rd St., telephone # 8-7646, managed by Malcolm Aitken.

866 Some time after teaming up with Elvis and Scotty Moore, Bill Black also worked for Ace Appliance Co. It was located at 3431 Summer Ave. and was owned by Robert G. Kinkle and Luther E. Gatlin.

867 There was an Elvis L. Lovell living in Memphis in 1950. He was a clerk at Longhill Fisheries and lived with wife, Alma, at 1759 Jackson Ave. Oddly enough, Alma Lovell was the saleswoman at Delta Record Distribution Co., which distributed Elvis's "That's All Right (Mama)" in 1955.

868 Elvis loved to drink "purple cows," a mixture of grape soda and vanilla ice cream.

869 Elvis reportedly sang for the US Armed Forces at the Brigadier General James M. Kennedy Hospital in 1953.

870 Elvis's favorite club in 1953 and 1954 was Doc's, located ten miles from Memphis in Frayser, Tennessee.

871 Elvis owned a pair of clear plastic shoes in the early 1950's.

872 When Elvis walked into the Memphis Recording Service on July 18, 1953, the first person he met was Marion Keisker, Sam Phillips' secretary.

873 Marion Keisker kept a handwritten studio log in red spiral-bound notebooks at the studio. After Elvis left the Memphis Recording Service with his acetate she wrote in her notebook: "Elvis Pressley— good ballad singer—462 Alabama Street—37-4185."

874   Sam Phillips was heavily in debt around the time Elvis first walked into his studio. He almost lost the recording service company.

875   The Memphis Recording Service offices were lined with white acoustic tile. The control room measured 12' X 17'. The main recording room was slightly bigger at 17' X 20'.

876   The Memphis Recording Service created products on disc, tape, and wire. They also provided services involving air check, programs, spot sales, microgroove, acetate masters, metal processing, 33 1/3 rpm, 45 rpm, and 78 rpm.

877   During the early to mid-1950's, there were only two record labels in Memphis. They were the Bihari Brothers' Modern/RPM label and Sam Phillips's Sun label.

878   Elvis's second recording at the Memphis Recording Service in 1953 resulted in an acetate with "It Wouldn't Be the Same Without You" on the B-side.

879   In 1953 and 1954, Elvis got his hair cut at Blake's Coiffure Shop located at Poplar and Lauderdale in Memphis. Blake Johnson, the shop's owner, trimmed Elvis's hair on several occasions.

880   Red West was number 36 on the L.C. Humes High School senior football squad during the 1954-1955 school year. He was a year younger than Elvis and graduated from high school in 1954.

881   Richard Earl Stanley was born on December 13, 1953, in Huntsville, Alabama. His parents were Dee and Bill Stanley. When Vernon Presley married Dee, Richard became Elvis's step-brother.

882 In December of 1953, Sam Phillips officially started Sun Studios.

883 When it first opened, Sun Studios had five microphones and a single-track, mono-input board.

884 Gladys Presley earned $4 a day and wore an aqua uniform while working at St. Joseph's Hospital in Memphis. Elvis walked his mother home from work at St. Joseph's every night.

885 Elvis bought some of his record albums from Charlie's Record Store on North Main Street in Memphis. Charles Hazelgrove was the store's owner.

886 Elvis recorded "That's When Your Heartaches Begin" on January 4, 1954, on an acetate at the Memphis Recording Service.

887 In February of 1954, Sam Phillips established the Hi-Lo Music Publishing Company.

888 In 1954, at 19 years of age, Elvis applied for a job as a Memphis policeman. He was turned down because he was too young.

889 Jeffery Beaulieu, Priscilla's second half-brother, was born in the spring of 1954.

890 On July 2, 1954, Elvis attended the funeral held at the Ellis Auditorium for R.W. Blackwood of the gospel group The Blackwood Brothers, who had been killed in an airplane crash in Alabama.

891 Dr. Jonas Salk developed the Salk vaccine in 1954. Elvis publicly took the vaccination in 1956 to help promote the "Fight Against Polio" campaign.

892 Before Sam Phillips paired Scotty Moore and Bill Black with Elvis, Scotty and Bill were members of a group called The Starlight Wranglers. The other band members were Doug Poindexter, Clyde Rush, and Millard Yow.

893 Scotty Moore and Bill Black quit the band The Starlight Wranglers after being paired with Elvis.

894 On July 4, 1954, Elvis met Scotty Moore and Bill Black at Scotty's house, located at 983 Belz Street in Memphis. It was a quadruplex.

895 During the course of their first meeting, Elvis, Scotty Moore, and Bill Black played "I Don't Hurt Anymore," "I Really Don't Want to Know," and "I Apologize."

896 Elvis's first professional recording at Sun Studios occurred on July 5, 1954.

897 At the time he began working with Elvis, Bill Black was married to a woman named Evelyn. They had three children: Nancy, Louis, and Leigh Ann.

898 Bill Black and his family lived at 971 Belz Street in Memphis, just a few doors away from Scotty Moore.

899 At the time Sam Phillips signed Elvis with Sun Records, he also owned the FLIP label.

900 On July 5, 1954, Elvis recorded his first "real" song for Sun Records, "That's All Right (Mama)."

901 Sam Phillips recorded Elvis with an Ampex 350C reel-to-reel tape deck with three 7-inch reel heads.

902 The serial number of the Ampex 350C machine at Sun Studios was 54L-220. It was made in Redwood City, California.

903 Sam Phillips used Scotch magnetic tape to record Elvis at Sun Studios.

904 Sam Phillips used an RCA Consolette monaural mixing console 76-D to mix all of Elvis's records.

905 When Sam Phillips signed Elvis as a Sun Studio recording artist in 1954, the Korean War was over.

906 Gladys and Vernon co-signed Elvis's contract with Sun Studios. Bob Neal was also present when Elvis signed with Sun Studios.

907 Elvis recorded "Blue Moon of Kentucky" during his second recording session at Sun, shortly after 7 p.m. on July 6, 1954.

908 In the 1950's, Scotty Moore's brother, Carney, owned a laundromat called University Park Cleaners, located at 613 McLean Blvd. in Memphis.

909 Jud Phillips, Sam's brother, handled all the promotion for Sun Studios. Jud had at one time been a gospel performer, a production assistant for Jimmy Durante, and a front man for Roy Acuff.

910 When Sam Phillips' brother, Jud, worked at WREC Radio in Memphis, he sang with the Jollyboys Quartet. WREC was affiliated with CBS radio.

911 When Elvis recorded at Sun Studios, he frequented Taylor's Restaurant, located next door to Sun at 710 Union Avenue. The phone number there was JA6-9505.

The Blue Moon Boys: Scotty Moore, Elvis Presley, and Bill Black.

912 Sam Phillips made acetate demos of Elvis's "That's All Right (Mama)" for the big DJs in town: Dewey Phillips (WHBQ), "Uncle Richard" (WMPA), and "Sleepy-Eyed" John Lepley (WHHM).

913 One of the first copies of Elvis's "That's All Right (Mama)" was sent to Paul Ackerman, music director of Billboard magazine.

914 Dewey Phillips's "Red, Hot and Blue" radio show aired from 9:00 p.m. to midnight on WHBQ from the Chiska Hotel, located at Main Street and Linden Avenue in Memphis.

915 Dewey Phillips was married to a woman named Dorothy. They had two sons, Randy and Jerry, and lived in Aloma, Tennessee.

916 Dewey Phillips was the first DJ to play Elvis's first record, "That's All Right (Mama)." It aired on July 10, 1954, at 9:30 p.m. as background music for a commercial.

917 When Dewey Phillips played Elvis's record, he introduced him as "Elton Preston!"

918 By the end of the night on July 10, 1954, Dewey Phillips had played Elvis's "That's All Right (Mama)" twelve times!

919 WHHM Radio was broadcast from the Sterick Building in Memphis. Disc Jockey "Sleepy-Eyed" John Lepley was the first to play Elvis's "Blue Moon of Kentucky" on air in July 1954. He was credited with playing Elvis's first country and western song, while Dewey Phillips played Elvis's first rhythm and blues song.

920 After his "That's All Right (Mama)" became the most requested song in Memphis, Elvis was quoted as saying, "I was scared to death. I was shaking all over when I heard what happened. I just couldn't believe it, but Dewey kept telling me to 'cool it.' It was really happening!"

921   The day after Dewey Phillips first played Elvis's "That's All Right (Mama)," Sam Phillips received an order for 6,000 advance copies!

922   Dewey Phillips received a lot of flack from other disc jockeys for playing Elvis's music on his program.

923   On July 12, 1954, Sam Phillips ordered 1,000 45 rpm and 1,000 78 rpm records of Elvis's "That's All Right (Mama)" to be pressed by Plastic Products, a local company owned by Robert E. "Buster" Williams.

924   On July 12, 1954, Scotty Moore became Elvis's new manager. A one page contract was signed by both parties, stipulating that Elvis got 50% and Bill and Scotty each got 25%. Scotty also got a 10% commission as Elvis's manager for any gig he booked.

925   Popular Tunes ran the first ad for Elvis's record in July of 1954.

926   Ruben Cherry (b. January 30, 1922), owner of The Home of the Blues Record Shop at 107 Beale Street in Memphis, was the first to stock Elvis's "That's All Right (Mama)" record.

927   On July 19, 1954, Elvis's "That's All Right Mama" 45rpm record arrived in record stores.

928   Ruben Cherry, manager of The Home of the Blues Record Shop in Memphis, lent Elvis money several times so that Elvis could get to his shows. Ruben lived at 606 S. Lauderdale.

929 On July 19, 1954, Stan Kesler delivered a small order of Elvis's new record to the Charles Record Store, located on Main Street in Memphis.

930 The Home of The Blues Record Shop was owned by the same people who owned the Southern Amusement Company. The owners, Clarence A. and Celia Camp, lived at 630 Madison Ave. The store was located at 107 Beale Street; the phone number was 5-6303.

931 It was reported that, at 9:00 a.m. on July 19, 1954, fifteen-year-old Eldene Beard became the first person to purchase a copy of Elvis's "That's All Right (Mama)," from the Charles Record Store.

932 Elvis's "That's All Right (Mama)" sold over 7,000 copies in Memphis during the first few weeks of its release—and Sam Phillips hadn't even had that many copies pressed yet!

933 Over 20,000 copies of Elvis's "That's All Right (Mama)" sold in the Memphis area alone in 1954.

934 On July 23, 1954, Alta Hayes of the Big State Record Distributors became the first to place a large order for Elvis's new record. This company was responsible for introducing Elvis's "That's All Right (Mama)"/"Blue Moon of Kentucky" to other cities and states.

935 Elvis had his first press interview on July 27, 1954, with Edwin Howard of the *Memphis Press-Scimitar* for his "Front Row" column. The interview was conducted during Elvis's lunch break at Crown Electric.

936 A five paragraph article ran in the July 28, 1954, issue of the *Memphis Press-Scimitar*. In it, Elvis was called "An Overnight Sensation." The newspaper was headquartered at 495-501 Union Avenue. The newspaper's general manager was Enoch Brown, editor

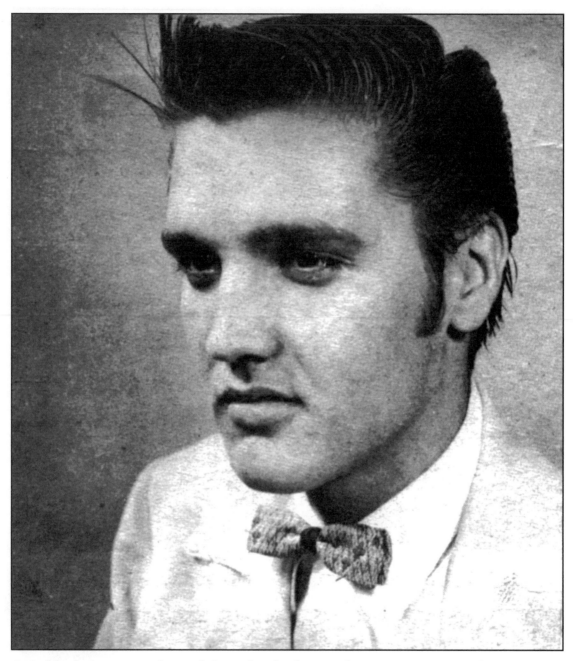

One of the first important photos of Elvis, taken for the Memphis Press-Scimitar. *Used in conjunction with a story written by Edwin Howard for his Front Row column on July 27, 1954.*

was E.J. Meeman, and managing editor was J.Z. Howard. The phone number at the paper was 8-2141.

937 Edwin Howard, the first reporter who interviewed Elvis, lived at 1355 Linden Avenue, Apt. 45 with his wife, Olivia.

938 Bob Neal first met Elvis at the Overton Park Shell, located at 1928 Poplar Avenue in Memphis, on July 30, 1954.

939 Bob Neal's wife, Helen, first brought Elvis to Bob's attention. Elvis asked Helen for encouragement and reassurance in regards to his singing and also asked if she thought he was good enough to act. Helen and Bob had five children.

940 Elvis's records were distributed in Florida by the Binkley Distributing Company. Binkley was located at 504 Delwood Avenue in Jacksonville, Florida.

941 Elvis became friends with Memphis policeman Robert Ferguson after meeting him at the Eagle's Nest Club in 1954.

942 Elvis loved to take girls to K's Drive-In during the 1950's, where he always ordered the same thing: cheeseburgers and milk shakes. K's was located at 166 Crump Blvd. E. in Memphis.

943 The owners of K's Drive-In were Dave C. Zanone, Jr. and Alyne Williams. Dave C. Zanone, Jr. lived at 3166 Kimball Ave.

944 Employees at K's Drive-In in the 1950's included cooks Thomas A. Craig (286 Union Ave.) and Sam Parham (661 E. McLemore), and James Dillard (267 E. Trigg Ave.), Sadie Greer (410 Edith Ave.), Mary Young (1598 Waverly) and Alma Callicutt (276 E. Waldorf),

who were part of the wait staff.

945 Elvis once won a small china boat at a milk bottle toss game at the Cotton Carnival in Memphis.

946 The biggest department store in Memphis was Goldsmith's Department Store, which had five floors. The fifth floor included a dining room with a 1,000-seat restaurant. There was also a separate men's dining room featuring a men's fashion show which Elvis reportedly attended once or twice in the 1950's.

947 On August 4, 1954, Elvis received a paycheck from Crown Electric in the amount of $42.51. The check number was 3968.

948 Elvis was interviewed by Buddy Bain for WMCA Radio in Corinth, Mississippi, in August of 1954.

949 Ed Parker began teaching Kempo at the Provo Health Club in 1954.

950 For the week ending August 18, 1954, Elvis's "Blue Moon of Kentucky" was at #3 on the Memphis music charts.

951 On August 31, 1954, Elvis was interviewed by Tom Perryman for KSIJ Radio in Gladewater, Texas.

952 On September 10, 1954, Elvis recorded "Just Because"/"Blue Moon" at Sun Studios.

953 In 1954 and 1955, Elvis ate bacon, lettuce, and tomato sandwiches morning, noon, and night.

954 Bill Fitzgerald of Williams Music Sales One Stop was a distributor of Elvis's records.

955 Elvis ate barbecued chicken only from Culpepper's Chicken Shack, located at 204 Hernando Street in Memphis. Walter Culpepper was the owner.

956 Bill Black wrecked Elvis's Lincoln in Arkansas. He fell asleep at the wheel and ran under a hay truck at full speed; the top of the car was pulled open like a tin can.

957 Dewey Phillips wanted to expose Elvis to some of the influential people in the music industry, so he took him to the Variety Club in the Gayoso Hotel where people in show business hung out.

958 Gladys Presley's best friend in Memphis was Willie Jane Nichols.

959 From August to October of 1954, Elvis frequented the 81 Club located on North Second Street in Memphis.

960 In mid-1954, Elvis gave Bob Neal a six month trial period to see if he was the right man to manage Elvis's new career.

961 Bob Neal arranged for Elvis to buy a car in 1954. Since Elvis did not have credit, he bought a 1951 Lincoln Continental on Bob's credit. The car had 10,000 miles on it. Elvis had "Elvis Presley—Sun Records" painted on the doors.

962 It was Bob Neal who suggested the name Blue Moon Boys for Elvis, Scotty Moore, and Bill Black in 1954.

963 Elvis and Bob Neal had many disagreements over music. Neal wanted Elvis to be strictly country according to Nashville standards. Elvis hated it and wanted to do record rock songs like "Good Rockin' Tonight" and "Baby Let's Play House."

964 Audubon Park in Memphis was built in 1954.

965 Red West went to Jones Junior College on a football scholarship in September of 1954.

966 While in college, Red West played at the Junior Rose Bowl in Pasadena, California.

967 After college, Red West joined the U.S. Marine Corps.

968 Red West was a musician. He played the trumpet and could read and write music.

969 Red West's mother, Lois, lived in Meridian, Mississippi.

970 Marion Keisker wrote one verse of "I Don't Care if the Sun Don't Shine," which Elvis recorded on September 10, 1954. Elvis cut the song in three takes.

971 Elvis recorded "I'll Never Let You Go," "Good Rockin' Tonight," and "Tomorrow Night" on September 10, 1954.

972 Because of the success of Elvis's first record, Sun Studios pressed 4,000 copies of his second effort, "I Don't Care if the Sun Don't Shine"/"Good Rockin' Tonight."

973   Elvis's "I Don't Care if the Sun Don't Shine"/"Good Rockin' Tonight" was released on September 25, 1954. By October, 4,000 copies had been sold.

974   In October of 1954, Elvis recorded "Give Me More, More, More (of Your Kisses)." The recording was never released.

975   DJ Fontana became Elvis's drummer at the Louisiana Hayride in late October of 1954. He used Gretsch drums.

976   The first commercial Elvis did was for the Southern Maid Donut Company, for a radio broadcast during one of his Louisiana Hayride appearances. The donut company, which distributed throughout the southeastern United States, was located at 1641 Union Avenue in Memphis, and its phone number was 7-2727.

977   It was Horace Logan of the Louisiana Hayride who first contacted Colonel Tom Parker about Elvis. Logan invited Parker to the Hayride to see Elvis perform.

978   In mid-October of 1954, Elvis, Scotty Moore, and Bill Black welcomed DJ Fontana into their Blue Moon Boys group.

979   Elvis, Scotty Moore, and Bill Black could not read music. They all played by ear.

980   In late 1954, Elvis and his parents moved into a two-story brick house located at 2414 Lamar Avenue in Memphis. They lived in the two-bedroom, bungalow-style house until mid-1955. Their telephone number was 37-4185.

Elvis and his second manager, Bob Neal.

981   Before Elvis and his family moved to the house at 2414 Lamar Avenue, Rupert R. and Annie Bloodworth lived there. Rupert was a painter.

982   From the early to mid-1950's, the Presleys' name was misspelled in the telephone directory as "Preseley."

983   One of the Presleys' neighbors when they lived on Lamar Avenue in Memphis was the Baker family.

984   By November of 1954, Elvis had quit his job at Crown Electric and signed with the Louisiana Hayride. At the time he left Crown, he had been promoted to the front office where his job was to answer the phones.

985   On November 15, 1954, Elvis received his first royalty check for his first record, "That's All Right (Mama)," in the amount of $82.50!

986   As per his contract with Sun Records, Elvis received a 3% royalty for every record sold.

987   Michelle Beaulieu, Priscilla's half-sister, was born in late 1954.

988   Sometime in late 1954, Sam Phillips became partners with Kemmons Wilson, founder of the Holiday Inn hotel chain. They started the first all-female radio station, WHER Radio.

989   Sam Phillips reportedly introduced Elvis to Lamar Fike in 1954. At that time, Phillips was teaching Fike how to be a disc jockey. Fike became one of Elvis's bodyguards.

990   Elvis recorded "Milkcow Blues Boogie" at Sun Studios on December 10, 1954.

991   In the 1950's, Elvis loved to wear black or white buck shoes or penny loafers.

992   Elvis went to a club called The Busy Betty on Lamar Avenue in Memphis in the early 1950's.

993   The Dorsey's *Stage Show* debuted on TV in the summer of 1954 as a replacement for *The Jackie Gleason Show*. Elvis appeared on *Stage Show* in 1956.

994   Elvis recorded "I'm Left, You're Right, She's Gone" at Sun Studios on December 18, 1954. He also recorded a slower version of the song entitled, "My Baby's Gone."

995   Ed Parker married Leilani Yap in Salt Lake City, Utah, on December 28, 1954. They would eventually have five children and fourteen grandchildren.

996   Scotty Moore got out of his managerial contract with Elvis on January 1, 1955.

997   Elvis made Bob Neal his official manager on January 1, 1955. Bob got 15%.

998   Elvis Presley Enterprises was first established by Elvis and Bob Neal after January of 1955. The main office was located in the Strick Building at 160 Union Avenue in Memphis.

999   The phone number for both Bob Neal and Elvis Presley Enterprises was 8-3667.

1000   Bob Neal's home phone number was 4-4029.

1001   Both Gladys and Vernon Presley liked Bob Neal and felt that he was honest.

1002   Even though Elvis had Bob Neal as his manager, he still actively participated in publicizing himself and his career.

1003   Elvis's "Milkcow Blues Boogie"/"You're a Heartbreaker" 45 rpm record was issued on January 8, 1955—Elvis's 20th birthday!

1004   "Milkcow Blues Boogie"/"You're a Heartbreaker" was never mentioned in Billboard magazine and as a result did not sell well.

1005   In 1955, Jud Phillips bought out Jim Bulleit's share of Sun Studios.

1006   Jack Clement was Sam Phillips' chief engineer at Sun Studios.

1007   Charlie Underwood (b. November 12, 1919) was Sun's A&R (Artist and Repertory) director.

1008   Dean Nichopoulos was born to Dr. Nick and his wife Edna in 1955. Dr. Nick was Elvis's doctor in the 1970's.

1009   Elvis and many of the blues singers from Memphis ate at Johnny Mills Barbecue Restaurant, located at Beale and 4th Street. It was a popular spot in Memphis at the time.

1010   In the early 1950's, Bill Perry was the Presleys' newspaper delivery boy.

1011   Some time in the mid-1950's, Elvis's cousin, Gene Smith, was stricken with polio. Because of this, Elvis later supported the March of Dimes organization.

1012 Whenever Elvis hugged or kissed his grandmother, Minnie Mae, she playfully slapped him away.

1013 Mrs. Margaret Sutton was the photographer for Elvis's first publicity photo shoot, which occurred at the Blue Light Studio in January of 1955. The studio is still open today.

1014 The Blue Light Studio is located at 130 Beale Street in Memphis. At the time of Elvis's first photo shoot, the studio was owned by Frank G. Link (b. March 12, 1882) and his wife, Corrie. Frank and Corrie lived at 1266 Castalia. The manager of the studio was Elizabeth P. Waddell, who lived at 179 Gilbert.

1015 It was rumored that when Elvis was in New York City on January 18, 1955, he bought a Corvette from Don Allen Chevrolet at a cost of $3,804.

1016 In January of 1955, Elvis was interviewed by Lynn McDowell for WBIP Radio in Booneville, Mississippi.

1017 In the mid-1950's, Elvis wore Fruit-of-the-Loom underwear in size 32-34.

1018 In 1955, Elvis weighed a mere 160 pounds! Gladys forced him to gain weight because she felt he was too skinny and unhealthy looking.

1019 In the 1950's, Elvis shaved every other day.

1020 Dixie Peach Pomade was Elvis's favorite hair dressing in the late 1950's. Elvis also favored Presto hairspray and Lustre Creme Concentrate shampoo.

1021 After only a few months of fame, Elvis presented his friend Red West with a gift of a 1926 Ford Model A that cost Elvis $125.00.

1022 Elvis Presley Enterprises was first listed in the Memphis telephone directory in February of 1955.

1023 Music Sales distributed Sun records throughout Tennessee in the 1950's. They were located at 117 Union Avenue in Memphis.

1024 In the mid-1950's, Bill Williams was the publicist for Sun Records.

1025 In 1954 and 1955, Elvis answered his own fan mail. He stopped only when the hectic touring began and the mail count hit over 500 letters per week.

1026 On February 5, 1955, Robert Johnson of the *Memphis Press-Scimitar* was responsible for the first editorial coverage of Elvis without benefit of an interview.

1027 Elvis first met Colonel Tom Parker at Palumbo's, a Memphis coffee shop, on February 6, 1955.

1028 On February 14, 1955, Colonel Parker began helping Bob Neal with Elvis's career.

1029 Vernon's social security number was 425-26-8732. He signed the card "Vernon E. Pressley."

1030 Colonel Parker first helped Elvis and his manager, Bob Neal, by getting Elvis booked in Carlsbad, New Mexico.

1031 In their March 1955 issue, *Country and Western* magazine became the first periodical to feature a photo of Elvis and a story on his budding career.

Elvis waxing his prized possession: his first Cadillac.

1032 On March 14, 1955, while en route to New York City to do the *Arthur Godfrey's Talent Scout Show*, Elvis stopped in Washington, DC to be interviewed by Jimmy Dean for his "Town and Country Jubilee" show on WMAL Radio.

1033 In March of 1955, Elvis, Scotty Moore, and Bill Black traveled to New York City to audition for the *Arthur Godfrey's Talent Scouts Show*. Arthur Godfrey said that he did not like Elvis's appearance and that Elvis had too much acne. Godfrey liked the artists who appeared on his show to have clean, blemish-free skin. Elvis and his band were turned down!

1034 Disc jockey Bill Randle was offered the chance to meet Elvis in March of 1955, but declined because he did not want to be on the road at the time.

1035 The Binkley Distribution Company's first order for Elvis's "Baby Let's Play House" was 300 copies, while the Big State Record Distributors in Dallas, Texas, ordered 500 copies.

1036 With a $200 royalty check from Sun Studios, Elvis bought his mother a dress and a good pair of shoes. Gladys's feet were so swollen that day, however, that she could not try the shoes on.

1037 In 1955, Gladys was quoted as saying, "Elvis would hear us worrying about our debts; being out of work and sickness and so on. He would say, 'Don't you worry none. When I grow up, I'm going to buy you a house and pay everything you owe at the grocery store and get two Cadillacs; one for you and Daddy and one for me.' Little as he was he'd look up at me holding onto my skirt and you know, I'd believe him!"

1038 Biff Collie, a disc jockey from Houston, Texas, interviewed Elvis in 1955.

1039 The first photograph of Elvis singing was printed in the Booneville, Mississippi, *Banner* in 1955.

1040 Gladys Presley had her hair cut and styled by Mr. Tommy at Goldsmith's Department Store in the mid-1950's. In addition, Mrs. Johnny Crabb sometimes styled Gladys's hair in a beauty parlor.

1041 At 4:45 p.m. on April 3, 1955, Elvis received a speeding ticket from Officer Strange, badge number 262, in Caddo Parish, Louisiana. Elvis was driving his pink and white 1954 Cadillac at the time. The county jailer in Caddo Parish was Ralph Ferris. In his report, he stated that Elvis was stopped for speeding "in TVT Patrol" on US 171 on April 3, 1955.

1042 The license plate on Elvis's pink and white 1954 Cadillac was 2D-35218 (Tennessee).

1043 Elvis was to appear in court on April 5, 1955, for his arraignment for speeding. A bond of $25 was paid in cash at the District Attorney's office.

1044 *LIFE* magazine was the first to do a feature story on Elvis after conducting an interview with him in Amarillo, Texas, on April 19, 1955.

1045 Elvis's 1954 Cadillac caught fire while on the road in Texarkana, Arkansas, during the last week of April, 1955.

1046 Elvis visited the Roanoke Record Shop, located at 116 W. Church Avenue in Roanoke, Virginia, on May 5, 1955. The store was owned by Mrs. Viola Bess.

1047 Elvis bought R&B records at The Home of the Blues record store in Memphis.

1048 In mid-1955, when Elvis asked his mother if he was vulgar on stage, Gladys replied, "You're puttin' too much into your singin', though you're not vulgar. But you keep that kind of activity and you won't live to be thirty!"

1049 In response to being called vulgar on stage, Elvis was quoted as saying, "That hurt me bitter. God gave me my voice. I've never danced vulgar in my life. I've just been jigglin'."

1050 It was rumored that Elvis approached F. "Yankie" Barhanovich to be his manager. Yankie was well known in the music business at the time, and his daughter, Ann Raye, was a Decca label artist.

1051 Jimmy Velvet met Elvis in Jacksonville, Florida, on May 13, 1955. Velvet was a freshman in high school at the time. He became the owner of several Elvis Presley museums throughout the United States.

1052 Elvis was interviewed by Ted Crutchfield for WCMS Radio in Norfolk, Virginia, on May 17, 1955. Elvis's "Blue Moon of Kentucky" played on the jukebox throughout the interview, which was recorded on a 16-inch recording disc. Reportedly, Crutchfield still has the disc!

1053 Elvis made a special appearance on *The Roy Orbison Show* on May 31, 1955.

1054 In June of 1955, *Cowboy Songs* magazine became the first to feature a full article about Elvis. It was entitled, "Sun's Newest Star."

1055 In June of 1955, Bob Neal sent Elvis to the Speer Studio to have some publicity portraits made. The studio was owned by William and Vancil Speer.

1056 Vancil Speer coerced Elvis into taking his shirt off for some sexy photos during the June 1955 Speer Studio photo shoot. Those photos are extremely popular today.

1057 The portraits of Elvis taken at Speer Studio in June of 1955 were taken with a German Goerzdader camera.

1058 From June of 1955 until May 11, 1956, Elvis and his family rented a house at 1414 Getwell Street. Their phone number was 48-4921.

1059 Sixteen-year-old Jack Baker was Elvis's neighbor in 1955.

1060 Colonel Parker reportedly approached Gladys and Vernon at the 1414 Getwell Street house about signing Elvis with him.

1061 Gladys Presley hated Tom Parker and made sure he knew just how she felt.

1062 Some time in 1955, Elvis recorded the song "Sunshine" at Sun Studios, but it was never released.

1063 Both Elvis and his mother had a fear of flying. When Elvis had to fly while touring, Gladys got very upset and prayed for her son until she knew he was safe.

1064 Elvis visited the Flamingo, a nightclub for R&B singers and performers, in 1955.

1065 In July of 1955, Scotty Moore traded his famous Gibson ES 295 guitar for an LS model.

1066 On July 6, 1955, the Annual Country & Western Popularity Poll was established. Organized by Bobby Ritter of WTUP Radio in Tupelo, Mississippi, the contest included votes from sixteen states. Elvis was chosen #1 by ten states!

1067 In 1955, Sam Phillips fought country promoters who thought Elvis was going to ruin country music.

1068 Elvis recorded "Mystery Train" at Sun Studios on July 11, 1955. There were no drums on the original recording; they were added at the last minute by Johnny Bernero.

1069 On July 14, 1955, Elvis borrowed money from Colonel Parker so he could make a car payment on his Lincoln to keep it from being repossessed. The Colonel wrote Elvis a check for $33. Elvis cashed the check at Vennucci's Liquor Store in Memphis.

1070 Since 1955, the TV News Archives at Vanderbilt University Library in Nashville, Tennessee, has kept copies of every piece of news coverage on Elvis Presley. This collection process continued even after Elvis's death.

1071 On August 15, 1955, Colonel Parker took Elvis, Gladys, Vernon, Bob Neal and his wife, Hank Snow, and Sam Phillips to an expensive dinner at the Peabody Hotel. Parker invited Snow in hopes that Snow's presence might convince Gladys to allow Elvis to sign with him.

1072 On August 15, 1955, after getting his mother's approval, Elvis signed a contract with the infamous Colonel Tom Parker.

Elvis standing on Beale Street in Memphis with several store owners, including the Lansky brothers.

1073 The contract between Elvis and the Colonel stipulated that Parker was a "special advisor" to Elvis and his career. The contract was for a duration of one year with a two year extended option. Both Vernon and Gladys had to sign the contract as Elvis was not yet of legal age.

1074 Tom Parker was 40 years old and Elvis was 20 when they signed the contract in 1955.

1075 When Colonel Parker got the William Morris Agency to book Elvis in 1955-1956, there were rumors that there was never a formal agreement or contract signed between the three parties. Everything was agreed to by handshakes.

1076 X Records, a subsidiary of RCA-Victor managed by Joe Delaney, was interested in signing Elvis in 1955. When Bob Neal quoted Elvis's price, Delaney said no thanks!

1077 According to Jerry Schilling, he met Elvis some time in 1955 at one of Elvis's football games at the Community Center in Memphis. Schilling became a member of Elvis's entourage.

1078 Gladys saw a pink Cadillac being driven by the husband of a patient at St. Joseph's Hospital and decided she'd like one for herself. Elvis made his mother's wish come true.

1079 The first car Elvis bought his mother was a 1954 Ford, not a pink Cadillac. Elvis had the car, which had a black top, painted pink.

1080 Earl Ridling was the owner of Earl's Hot Biscuits, one of the first drive-ins, which Elvis frequented in the 1950's.

1081 W.W. Herenton was the carhop who waited on Elvis most of the time at Earl's Hot Biscuits. Herenton went on to become the Mayor of Memphis.

1082 In 1955, Al Smith's Record Store in South Bend, Indiana, heavily advertised Elvis's records and established a mail order business to accommodate out of town customers.

1083 After representing Elvis, Bob Neal managed Johnny Cash.

1084 The Colonel had a tape of Elvis's delivered to famous disc jockey Bill Randle in August of 1955. Although Randle felt Elvis's music was not good enough to play in New York, he did play him in Cleveland, Ohio.

1085 On August 27, 1955, Elvis was interviewed by Bob Neal for his show on WMPS Radio in Memphis.

1086 David Edward Stanley was born in Fort Eustis, Virginia, on August 30, 1955, to Davada and Bill Stanley. David became Elvis's step-brother.

1087 On September 25, 1955, Ed Sullivan changed the name of his show from *Toast of the Town* to *The Ed Sullivan Show*.

1088 It was rumored that, in 1955, the Presleys lived in a house located at the corner of Kimball and Park Street in Memphis.

1089 Throughout Elvis's career, Colonel Parker lived in a house at 1221 Gallatin Road in Madison, Tennessee.

1090 Elvis bought himself a $175 Martin & Company guitar in late 1955. He had a special leather cover made for the guitar with his name engraved on it.

1091 It was rumored that the leather guitar cover that Elvis used in 1956 was made by one of his uncles, but this rumor is false.

1092 In 1956, Elvis made the following statement about his leather guitar cover: "There's only one other guitar in a case like that. Hank Snow has it. He gave me the idea. It keeps the guitar from getting splintered when I swing it around and it hits my belt buckle."

1093 From 1955 on, Colonel Parker's business address was Box 417, Madison, Tennessee. His phone number was 8-2858.

1094 In October of 1955, Sam Phillips filed an injunction against Duke Records, which was owned by Donald Robey.

1095 Dee Kilpatrick of Mercury Records offered to purchase Elvis's contract from Sun Studios in 1955 for the sum of $10,000, but was outbid by RCA-Victor.

1096 Sam Phillips approached Polish-owned Chess Records with an offer to have them buy all of his Sun label artists, including Elvis Presley, in the fall of 1955. Owners Leonard and Phil Chess said no.

1097 Elvis's Sun records never made it to the West Coast. Until RCA-Victor took over, he was virtually unknown in that part of the U.S.

1098 Sam Phillips designed Elvis's first Sun album and was making plans to release it in early 1956, but it never came to be. He was forced to sell Elvis's contract to pay his mounting debts.

1099 Sam Phillips held an auction for Elvis's Sun Records contract in mid-November of 1955. The auction was held at the Andrew Jackson Hotel in Nashville, Tennessee, and at the Warwick Hotel in New York City.

Elvis and his notorious manager, Colonel Tom Parker, in Parker's Madison, Tennessee, office, November 26, 1956.

1100   Colonel Parker received sole management rights to Elvis and his career after negotiating with Bob Neal at a November 1955 auction.

1101   Frank Walker, president of MGM Records, made an offer for Elvis's Sun Records contract and personally sent Sam Phillips a telegram asking about the price of the contract.

1102   Dot Records, founded by Randy Wood, offered $7,500 for Elvis's Sun Records contract in 1955.

1103   Columbia Records offered to buy Elvis's Sun Records contract for $15,000.

1104   Ahmet Ertegun, head of Atlantic Records, made a $25,000 offer for Elvis's Sun Records contract.

1105   After hearing Elvis on the radio, RCA-Victor executive Steve Sholes alerted RCA-Victor to this new sound. He was the person responsible for convincing RCA-Victor to purchase Elvis's Sun contract. At the New York auction on November 20, 1955, RCA-Victor made an offer of $35,000 for Elvis's Sun Records contract.

1106   When Sam Phillips sold Elvis's contract to RCA-Victor, he was promoting Elvis as a country & western singer.

1107   RCA-Victor's trademark was Nipper the dog sitting next to a 1905 Victor Gold Medal phonograph. Colonel Parker had a picture of Nipper sitting next to a hound wearing a hat on the wall of his office in Madison, Tennessee.

1108   RCA-Victor gave Steve Sholes one condition regarding signing Elvis with their label: Sholes had to personally guarantee that the advance money would be paid back within the first year! Sholes agreed to the terms and prayed for the best. Not only was the advance recouped, but RCA-Victor made a sizable profit as well.

1109 RCA-Victor did not have enough faith in Elvis's ability to actually guarantee the money for his contract, so the Colonel called the Aberbachs from Hill & Range Music Company and asked them to endorse Elvis, which they did. In turn, RCA signed Elvis.

1110 In addition to Elvis, the parties who signed Elvis's new contract with RCA-Victor were Vernon Presley, Sam Phillips, Colonel Parker, and RCA executive Coleman Tipley III. Elvis's contract was signed on November 20, 1955.

1111 RCA-Victor put up just $20,000 for Elvis's contract—$15,000 went to Sam Phillips and $5,000 to Elvis.

1112 Hill & Range put up the other $15,000 needed to conclude the RCA deal in exchange for a co-publishing deal with Phillips's Hi-Lo Music Publishing Company.

1113 Elvis was brought to the attention of Jean and Julian Aberbach by Hill & Range representative Grelun Landon, who saw Elvis in concert.

1114 RCA-Victor considered the $5,000 for Elvis an advance, but Colonel Parker conned them into giving it to Elvis as a "gift."

1115 As Sam Phillips demanded a total of $35,000 for himself for Elvis's contract, he put pressure on RCA-Victor by threatening to release Elvis's new record. When Colonel Parker used this as leverage and threatened to cancel the deal, RCA gave Parker the extra money rather than lose the deal.

1116 The contract that Parker and Elvis signed with RCA-Victor did not include an audit clause, effectively denying them access to accounting and sales reports.

1117 There were many rumors that Elvis's RCA-Victor contract stipulated that he was to be paid $1,000 a week for the next twenty years.

1118 According to the RCA-Victor contract, Elvis received a 5% royalty per record sold.

1119 Hill & Range owners Jean and Julian Aberbach had publishing rights to at least one side of each single Elvis recorded. Elvis was forced to pick one of their songs for one side of his singles for the rest of his life. Elvis received 50% of the song publishing royalties, and Jean and Julian Aberbach received 25% each.

1120 Hill & Range Music Company was located at 1650 Broadway in New York City.

1121 It was because of RCA-Victor that Elvis expanded his music from country & western to rhythm & blues and pop.

1122 Joan Deary was Steve Sholes's assistant at RCA-Victor.

1123 The only sheet music made while Elvis was with Sun Records was for "I Forgot To Remember To Forget" (Sun 223). It was published by Hi-Lo Music and printed by Edward B. Marks Music Corp. in Radio City, New York.

1124 Soon after Elvis signed with RCA-Victor, he and Red West met with the Aberbachs at the famous Brown Derby restaurant in New York City, where Jean and Julian explained Elvis's new publicity campaign and strategy.

1125 RCA-Victor assumed that the Elvis craze would die out after several more singles and two or three albums. How wrong they were!

1126 Elvis's first RCA-Victor release was "Mystery Train," in November of 1955.

1127 In 1955, Scotty Moore earned a little over $8,000 with RCA-Victor.

1128 Scotty Moore moved to 1248 Meda Street in Memphis, Tennessee, in late 1955 or early 1956.

1129 Bill Black moved to 4188 Pike's Peak Avenue around the same time that Scotty Moore moved to Meda Street in Memphis.

1130 In the 1950's, DJ Fontana lived in Shreveport, Louisiana.

1131 From the end of 1955 to mid-1956, Gladys baked a coconut cake for Elvis every day.

1132 A book by Alice Waller entitled *Nineteen Fifty-Five* is all about Elvis.

1133 Arthur Hooten worked with Elvis in the mid-1950's. Hooten's mother worked with Gladys at Britling's Cafeteria in Memphis.

1134 RCA-Victor presented Elvis with a Nipper the dog necktie, which he wore often and with pride.

1135 In the mid-1950's, Elvis's style of dress was always unique, even down to his belt, which he wore with the buckle to the left side.

1136 Elvis took Dewey Phillips to his dentist to have Dewey's teeth capped. The procedure cost Elvis $400!

1137   In the 1950's, Elvis owned a Smith-Corona typewriter by L.C. Smith. He used it to answer his fan mail.

1138   Elvis pawned his Martin D-18 guitar at the Nathan Novick Pawn Shop located at 131 Beale Street in Memphis.

1139   Colonel Parker hated Elvis's Southern drawl, as he felt it made it hard for people to understand him. Elvis also stuttered a lot. In late 1955, Colonel Parker forced Elvis to take speech classes with a certified therapist to help with his diction.

1140   From late 1955, Colonel Parker wore a gold ring with the initials 'TP' on the ring finger of his right hand.

1141   *Billboard* magazine featured two stories on Elvis in their December 3, 1956 issue. Both stories were about the new RCA-Victor contract. They were titled "Double Deals Hurt" and "Presley Into Stardom."

1142   In the December 5, 1955, issue of *Billboard* magazine, Elvis was featured in a full page ad.

1143   Hill & Range released the first folio of words and music to Elvis's songs on December 10, 1955. A photo of Elvis's parents was included on the back cover.

1144   Hill & Range helped Elvis establish Elvis Presley Music, Inc. They became 50/50 partners with Elvis for five years.

1145   In mid-December of 1955, Elvis was contracted to appear on the Dorsey's Stage Show. Stage Show was broadcast from CBS's Studio 50, located on Broadway between 53rd and 54th Streets in New York City.

Elvis and RCA-Victor executive and representative Steve Sholes.
It was Sholes who talked RCA-Victor into signing Elvis.

1146 The agreement between Elvis, the Colonel, and the Dorseys involved Elvis appearing on the *Stage Show* four times for $1,250 per show. Colonel Parker talked them into having Elvis on the program six times.

1147 James R. Denny, head of entertainment for the Grand Ole Opry, was named "*Billboard* Man of the Year" for 1955. Denny was the person who insulted Elvis when he appeared on the Opry.

1148 Elvis grossed $55,000 in earnings in 1955.

1149 Some time in the middle to late 1950's, Susan Johnson won "The Woman of the Year" award from the Tri Delta Sorority in Memphis. She was Elvis's teacher at L.C. Humes High School in 1949 and lived at 1259 Agnes.

1150 Some time in the mid-1950's, Colonel Parker suffered a minor heart attack.

1151 After his heart attack, the Colonel offered Elvis's contract to Oscar Davis, an agent who worked with him, for $100,000. Davis refused because he couldn't come up with that kind of money. Oscar Davis was known as "The Baron," and was a vaudeville performer from 1910-1917.

1152 Elvis and his parents were very careful with their investments in the early part of Elvis's career. They purchased only United States government bonds.

1153 Gladys enjoyed visiting old friends and "the gang" in Tupelo, Mississippi after Elvis's popularity soared. Her Sunday visits made her feel truly loved for herself and not for the fact that she was Elvis Presley's mother.

1154 Elvis was very shy and rarely granted interviews, unless Colonel Parker forced him.

1155 The Montreal, Canada, *Samedi-Dimanche* newspaper named Elvis the most popular singer of 1956. They even sent him a cake for his 22nd birthday in January of 1957.

1156 Elvis's first RCA recording session was held on January 10 and 11, 1956. The studio was located at 1520 McGavock Street in Nashville, Tennessee, in a building owned by the Methodist Church.

1157 Steve Sholes was Elvis's A&R man for his first RCA-Victor recording session.

1158 The following musicians were used for Elvis's first RCA recording session in January of 1956: guitar—Scotty Moore, Chet Atkins, Elvis Presley; bass—Bill Black; drums—DJ Fontana; piano—Floyd Cramer; vocals—Gordon Stoker, Ben and Brock Speer.

1159 Elvis recorded five songs on January 10th and 11th, 1956: "I Got A Woman," "Heartbreak Hotel," "Money Honey," "I'm Counting on You," and "I Was the One."

1160 It took Elvis over three hours to record a decent take of "Money Honey" on January 10, 1956.

1161 The January 1956 session was for Elvis's first RCA-Victor album, *Elvis Presley* (LPM-1254).

1162 When Elvis recorded at the RCA-Victor studio, Hill & Range sent him 100 demos. Out of those, he chose to cut only five or ten of the songs.

1163 Elvis wanted to record rock-n-roll, but RCA-Victor and Hill & Range offered him very limited material to work with. He was only allowed to record songs owned by Hill & Range.

1164 The Tree Publishing Company, located at 905 16th Avenue in Nashville, Tennessee, was founded in 1956 by Jack Stapp. One of the first songs they acquired the publishing rights to was Elvis's "Heartbreak Hotel."

1165 The first 14 songs Elvis recorded with RCA-Victor sold over a million copies each.

1166 Elvis made a personal appearance at the L.C. Humes High School "Father's Night Show" on Friday, January 13, 1956. He sang ten songs.

1167 After selling Elvis's Sun Studios contract to RCA-Victor, Sam Phillips and his family moved into a new house at 79 S. Mendenhall Road in Memphis.

1168 It was reported that the William Morris Agency set up the deal for Elvis to appear on the Dorsey's *Stage Show*.

1169 Abe Lastfogel, president of the William Morris Agency, helped Colonel Parker with Elvis's early career. He was Elvis's agent.

1170 Elvis and his band rehearsed every night for a week before their first appearance on the Dorsey's *Stage Show* on January 28, 1956. Elvis wanted their performance to be flawless.

1171 When RCA-Victor released Elvis's "Heartbreak Hotel" on January 27, 1956, they were shocked—the record bombed! Steve Sholes panicked about the poor sales. It wasn't until Elvis sang the song on TV that the sales skyrocketed.

1172 By January of 1956, Colonel Parker and RCA-Victor had dropped the Blue Moon Boys name from anything involving Elvis. The Colonel would not allow any of the Elvis Presley fan clubs to print photos of Bill or Scotty in their newsletters, magazines, or brochures.

1173 Early on January 27, 1956, Elvis arrived in New York City for the Dorsey's *Stage Show* rehearsals.

1174 The Dorsey's *Stage Show* was broadcast from CBS Studio 50, located at 1697 Broadway in New York City.

1175 While in New York, Elvis visited Times Square and purchased a $1 necktie at the Supreme Men's Shop.

1176 When Elvis was in New York City, he stayed at either the Warwick Hotel or the Essex House.

1177 When at the posh Warwick Hotel located at 65 West 54th Street, Elvis ate in the Raleigh Room and stayed in room 527.

1178 It was raining in New York City when Elvis made his first television appearance on the Dorsey's *Stage Show* on January 28, 1956.

1179 Cleveland disc jockey Bill Randle introduced Elvis on *Stage Show* on January 28, 1956.

1180 For his first appearance on *Stage Show*, Elvis sang "Shake, Rattle and Roll" with a "Flip, Flop and Fly" ending, and "I Got a Woman."

1181 The drummer who backed Elvis and his band during their first *Stage Show* performance was Louis Bellson. The piano player was Shorty Long.

1182 The TV crew for *Stage Show* said that singer Sarah Vaughn received more applause than Elvis or any other guest who appeared on the show.

1183 The Dorsey's *Stage Show* was sponsored by Railey's Appliance Center.

1184 *Stage Show* received an 18.4 rating with Elvis's first appearance.

1185 The mail received by the staff of *Stage Show* after Elvis's first appearance surpassed that of any other performer.

1186 Gladys was thrilled that Elvis was making so much money. She was finally able to pay bills on time and still have money left over.

1187 When Elvis was touring, he sent his mother money in the mail.

1188 One of the jewelers from whom Elvis purchased items in the 1950's was Harry Levitsch.

1189 In 1956, Elvis had this to say about the guitar: "I don't know how to play it well. I just carry it with me so I'll have something to do with my hands. I carry it for security, I guess. Gosh, I don't know that I could sing without a guitar in my hands."

1190 Elvis's guitar playing put people to work. His popularity caused an increased demand for instruments, which in turn caused guitar companies to hire more employees.

1191 Colonel Parker established the Mr. Songman Publishing Company in

Elvis with Tommy and Jimmy Dorsey during one of his latter appearances on the Dorsey's Stage Show.

1956. He received 40%, Elvis received 15%, and the remaining percentages went to other company executives.

1192 In addition to Mr. Songman Publishing Company, the Colonel opened several publishing companies for Elvis in 1956. They were Aaron Music, Elvis Music Inc., and Whitehaven Music.

1193 On January 30, 1956, Elvis gave his first big newspaper interview to Fred Danzig during a recording session at the RCA studios in New York.

1194 Elvis's second recording session with RCA occurred at their New York studio on January 30 and 31, 1956. The studio was located at 155 East 24th Street. The building is now a part of Baruch College.

1195 The following musicians were used for Elvis's second RCA recording session in January of 1956: guitar—Scotty Moore and Elvis Presley; bass—Bill Black; drums—DJ Fontana; piano—Shorty Long.

1196 The songs cut during the second RCA session in January of 1956 were "Blue Suede Shoes," "My Baby Left Me," "One-Sided Love Affair," "So Glad You're Mine," "I'm Gonna Sit Right Down and Cry," and "Tutti Frutti."

1197 The songs "Lawdy Miss Clawdy" and "Shake, Rattle and Roll" were recorded on February 3, 1956.

1198 In February of 1956, The Music Museum featured Elvis's RCA-Victor releases in their window.

1199 In the 1950's, Elvis was described as a cross between Johnny Ray and Marlon Brando.

1200 Elvis received a giant stuffed panda bear from Colonel Parker in 1956.

1201 Hairstylist Glenwood Dodgson of Grand Rapids, Michigan, is credited with creating an Elvis Presley haircut for fans.

1202 Elvis paid for George Klein's plastic surgery, a nose job, in 1956.

1203 Elvis made his second appearance on the Dorsey's *Stage Show* on February 4, 1956.

1204 During his second *Stage Show* appearance, Elvis was introduced by guest emcee Joe E. Brown.

1205 Elvis sang "Baby, Let's Play House" and "Tutti Frutti" during his second appearance on *Stage Show*.

1206 Kay Wheeler started the very first Elvis newsletter, *The Presley Press*.

1207 Elvis made his third appearance on the Dorsey's *Stage Show* on February 11, 1956.

1208 The guest emcee on *Stage Show* during Elvis's third appearance was Ella Fitzgerald.

1209 Elvis sang "Blue Suede Shoes" and "Heartbreak Hotel" during his third *Stage Show* appearance in 1956.

1210 On the February 11, 1956, episode of Dorsey's *Stage Show*, a trumpet player from the Dorsey orchestra played a solo during Elvis's "Heartbreak Hotel" segment, while a spotlight shown down on him.

1211 On the Dorsey's *Stage Show* in February of 1956, Elvis's guitar was out of tune. In addition, as Elvis was not used to a trumpet backup with this song, it caused him to be off on his timing.

1212 The producer of the Dorsey's *Stage Show* when Elvis performed was Al Span, the director was Frank Satenstein, and the assistant producer was Stanley Poss.

1213 In 1956, for every 89¢ Elvis Presley 45 rpm record purchased, Elvis received a 4.5¢ royalty.

1214 Elvis enjoyed cheeseburgers from Krystal, the South's answer to McDonald's, from the mid-1950's through the 1970's. Krystal was founded in 1932 by D.B. Davenport, Jr. and J. Glenn Sherrill.

1215 Elvis preferred the Krystal located at 135 Union Avenue in Memphis when he got a craving for a Krystal cheeseburger. He liked the service there better and thought the food tasted better as well.

1216 In February of 1956, "Heartbreak Hotel" sold 122,000 copies in one week.

1217 *The Hep Cat's Review* magazine featured an article entitled "Elvis Presley: Dig the Greatest!" in their February 1956 issue.

1218 On February 18, 1956, Elvis made his fourth appearance on the Dorsey's *Stage Show*.

1219 George DeWitt was the guest emcee during Elvis's fourth *Stage Show* appearance.

1220 During his fourth appearance on the Dorsey's *Stage Show*, Elvis sang "Tutti Frutti" and "I Was the One."

1221 When the hula-hoop became popular in the 1950's, Elvis couldn't do it at all!

1222 In 1956, Elvis made the following statement: "I know that the Lord can giveth and the Lord can taketh away. I might be herding sheep next year!"

1223 Barbecue was Elvis's favorite food, and when he got a craving for it he headed to Leonard's Barbecue, located at 1140 South Bellevue Blvd. in Memphis. The restaurant opened in 1956. Elvis's favorite meal at Leonard's consisted of shredded pork, beans, coleslaw, potato salad, and rolls. Meals were served "family-style," with big bowls and plates.

1224 Paulette Thomas created an Elvis Presley haircut for teens in 1956.

1225 *Billboard* magazine's March 3, 1956, headline read: "A Winnah! Presley Hot as $1 Pistol on Victor!"

1226 On March 7, 1956, a temporary, promotional envelope/sleeve was made for Elvis's "Blue Suede Shoes" (EPA-747). The record featured "Tutti Frutti," "I Got a Woman," and "Just Because," as well as the title song. There was a delay with the original shipment, so RCA-Victor sent the record out with the special sleeves.

1227 On March 8, 1956, Elvis was caught speeding on Kimball Street from Semmes to Lamar Avenue in Memphis. Later that day, he went to court to pay the fine.

1228 Richard Biondi, a Buffalo, New York, disc jockey, was fired on the air for playing an Elvis song during his program.

1229 Two-thirds of Elvis's first album, *Elvis Presley* (LPM-1254), was cut at Sun Studios. It was produced with a new "orthophonic" technique, which was a high fidelity recording process.

1230 *Elvis Presley* was released on March 13, 1956. It sold in stores for $3.98.

1231 Elvis's "Heartbreak Hotel" was not doing well in the spring of 1956, and RCA-Victor still wasn't convinced that he would be a success. To speed up production of his album, *Elvis Presley* (LPM-1254), RCA-Victor hired extra help. Their intention was to produce the album quickly, then dump Elvis.

1232 RCA-Victor released the first Elvis extended play album (EP), *Elvis Presley* (EPA-747), on March 13, 1956.

1233 Arnold Shaw, a music publicist, was hired by RCA-Victor to be Elvis's A&R man in the 1950's.

1234 In the late 1950's, RCA-Victor's regional representative in Memphis was Samuel Esgro.

1235 Colonel Parker officially became Elvis's manager on March 15, 1956.

1236 According to the new managerial contract, signed in March of 1956, Colonel Parker got 25% of Elvis's earnings.

1237 At the same time he signed Elvis, the Colonel also signed Scotty Moore, Bill Black, and DJ Fontana.

1238 Elvis appeared on the Dorsey's *Stage Show* for the fifth time on March 17, 1956.

Elvis with Mr. Television himself, Milton Berle, during his June 5, 1956 appearance on The Milton Berle Show.

1239 Just before he went to the *Stage Show* theater on March 17, 1956, Elvis had a jeweler come to the Warwick Hotel to show him several pieces of jewelry. It was on that day that Elvis bought his famous diamond horseshoe ring.

1240 During his fifth appearance on *Stage Show*, Elvis stayed in room 527 at the Warwick Hotel in New York.

1241 Comedian Henny Youngman was the guest emcee who introduced Elvis during his fifth appearance on the Dorsey's *Stage Show*.

1242 Elvis sang "Blue Suede Shoes" and "Heartbreak Hotel" during his March 17, 1956 *Stage Show* performance.

1243 Some time in the early part of 1956, Elvis traded in the 1942 Martin D-18 guitar, which he used in the beginning of his career with Sun Studios, at O.K. Houck & Company Music Shop. The store was located at 121 Union Avenue in Memphis.

1244 March 24, 1956 marked Elvis's sixth and final performance on the Dorsey's *Stage Show*.

1245 Before his final appearance of Dorsey's *Stage Show*, Elvis was introduced by comedian Jack E. Leonard.

1246 Elvis was interviewed by Carlton Brown at the Warwick Hotel after his last appearance on the *Stage Show*. In the interview, Elvis stated that his favorite song was "I Was the One."

1247 Colonel Parker hated Elvis's big, wide nose, his bad skin, and bad teeth. He thought that in order for Elvis to become a big star, he had to look the part.

1248 In late March of 1956, Elvis had plastic surgery. The operation was performed by Dr. Morry Parks, known as the "plastic surgeon to the stars." Dr. Parks eliminated the hump on Elvis's nose just below eye level, eliminated the dark shadows under Elvis's eyes, shortened the nose, and narrowed the nostrils. Elvis loved his new look.

1249 In 1956, Elvis started wearing caps on his teeth—both the front two as well as the teeth on each side of the front two. He did this because the side teeth looked too small in comparison to the capped middle teeth. Each porcelain cap cost $150.

1250 In early 1956, Elvis joined the American Guild of Variety Artists. His membership number was 165890.

1251 In the 1950's, Elvis favored peach ice cream, strawberry ice cream, and strawberry sodas.

1252 At the end of March 1956, Elvis took a train from Penn Station in New York City to Memphis, Tennessee. While waiting for the train, Elvis read a Sunday *Mirror* newspaper with the headline "2 Airliners Missing—127 Aboard."

1253 On March 24, 1956, Elvis bought a 3-wheel, black and red German Messerschmidt. The vehicle's ID number was 56007, its title number was 4447521, and its license plate number was 2-100222 (Tennessee). It weighed 3,600 pounds and got 50 miles per gallon.

1254 In March of 1956, RCA-Victor released Elvis's first double pocket EP, *Elvis Presley* (EPB-1254).

1255 *LIFE* magazine offered to feature Elvis on their cover in 1956, but

Colonel Parker promptly turned them down after finding out that they were unwilling to pay $150,000 for a picture of his "boy."

1256 Officials stated that juvenile delinquency rose 41% after Elvis became popular.

1257 RCA-Victor released Elvis's second EP, *Heartbreak Hotel* (EPA-821), in April of 1956.

1258 On April 2, 1956, it was determined that if Elvis got two more moving violations before March 8, 1957, his driver's license would be revoked. Elvis made sure to drive more carefully.

1259 In April of 1956, Elvis forfeited $51 when he failed to appear in traffic court on a speeding charge.

1260 In 1956, Ed Parker opened his first karate studio in Pasadena, California, with borrowed money. He had spent the previous year and a half teaching Utah police the art of karate. Parker became Elvis's Kempo instructor and good friend.

1261 Elvis appeared on *The Milton Berle Show* on April 3, 1956, in the hopes of boosting the show's falling ratings. The program was broadcast from aboard the USS Hancock in San Diego, California.

1262 Elvis sang "Shake, Rattle and Roll," "Heartbreak Hotel," and "Blue Suede Shoes" during his first appearance on *The Milton Berle Show*.

1263 During *The Milton Berle Show* in April of 1956, Elvis and Milton Berle performed a sketch where Berle played Elvis's twin brother, "Elvin."

Elvis sitting next to acquaintance Roberta Moore in a Memphis diner. Elvis ate Moore's sandwich and drank her milk per the instructions of a photographer; Moore subsequently sued Elvis for $47,500. The suit was settled out of court for $5,500.

1264 Milton Berle's orchestra leader was Victor Young.

1265 Elvis was paid $3,500 for his first appearance on *The Milton Berle Show*.

1266 Approximately 40 million people watched Elvis perform on *The Milton Berle Show* on April 3, 1956.

1267 On April 5, 1956, Elvis autographed his first arm. It belonged to Barbara Shepherd, a twelve-year-old from 2335 Seabreeze Drive in San Diego, California.

1268 On April 11, 1956, Elvis recorded "I Want You, I Need You, I Love You" at the RCA studio in Nashville, Tennessee. While en route to the session, there was a near disaster: Elvis's plane came within a few feet of the ground before the engine trouble was diagnosed and repaired.

1269 The following musicians were used for the April 11, 1956, recording session: guitar—Scotty Moore, Chet Atkins, and Elvis Presley; bass—Bill Black; drums—DJ Fontana; piano—Marvin Hughes; vocals—Gordon Stoker, Ben and Brock Speer.

1270 Elvis was interviewed by Jay Thompson in Breckenridge, Texas, on April 13, 1956, for KSTB Radio, Wichita Falls.

1271 Kay Wheeler met Elvis for the first time in San Antonio, Texas, on April 15, 1956. She organized the first national Elvis Presley Fan Club.

1272 Elvis was reportedly called "The King of Rock-n-Roll" for the first time by Bea Ramirez of the *Waco-News Tribune* on April 19, 1956. Ms. Ramirez wrote: "Shortly before he was to go on stage at the Heart O' Texas Coliseum, Elvis Presley, the new 21-year old, 'King of Rock-n-Roll' sat in a darkened Cadillac limousine for an interview—well hidden from the sight of 4,000 screaming, squealing teenagers, who were on hand to welcome him on Tuesday night. All the hep cats were there and not enough fuzz [police]!"

1273 Charlie Walker of WMAC Radio in San Antonio, Texas, interviewed Elvis on April 22, 1956.

1274 It was reported that Gladys and Vernon Presley were interested in purchasing the 1414 Getwell house in Memphis, but the owners were unwilling to sell to them. The Presleys were forced to move after bad feelings arose between the two parties; they quickly found a new home on Audubon Drive.

1275 In April of 1956, Elvis purchased a ranch-style house at 1034 Audubon Drive in Audubon Park, Memphis, for $40,000. Elvis and his family moved into their new house on May 11, 1956.

1276 As soon as the purchase of Elvis's Audubon Drive house was completed, Elvis had it insured with the Pidgeon-Thomas Insurance Agency. Frank Pidgeon was his broker.

1277 The Presleys were the only people in the Audubon Park neighborhood whose house had been paid for in full at the time of purchase.

1278 The Audubon Drive house was a one story ranch with pastel green boards, a gray roof, red brick trim, and white windows with black shutters. It had nine rooms, as well as a carport which led into the kitchen. It also had a fireplace and a piano.

1279 Elvis and his parents decorated the living room of their Audubon Drive home with wall-to-wall carpeting, dark wood paneling, bright floral drapes and Venetian blinds, modern couches, blonde wood chairs, a television, and a glass-topped coffee table. Elvis had red carpeting installed in the den.

1280 Elvis kept a photo of the Colonel on an end table in the living room of his Audubon Drive house.

1281 Elvis's bedroom had blue, orange, and yellow wallpaper; a pink floral bedspread with dust ruffle; a red phone; and several ceramic figurines.

1282 The swimming pool at the Audubon Drive house cost Elvis $10,000.

1283 Gladys got upset when Elvis fans clipped blades of grass from the lawn, collected water from the swimming pool, and stole milk bottles left for the milkman as souvenirs from the Audubon Drive house. In an attempt to keep his fans at bay and to give his family some privacy, Elvis had a wall and a gate with music notes installed around the property.

1284 Gladys Presley loved their first house. She was known to take a lawn chair down to the gates to sit and mingle with fans. She often posed for photos.

1285 Elvis hired Alberta Holman to cook and clean at the Audubon Drive house. He nicknamed her "Alberta VO-5" after the hair product.

1286 In 1956, Elvis became obsessed with Skil pool, a variation of French pool. He had a table set up at his new house.

1287 While living on Audubon Drive, Elvis had a black and white mixed breed terrier named Boy.

1288 Gladys Presley's best friends in Audubon Park were Mr. and Mrs. Nichols.

1289   Gladys Presley enjoyed showing off her silver service set for 100, a gift from her son.

1290   When fans visited the Audubon Drive house, Gladys Presley not only spent time with them, but sometimes even made them lunch.

1291   Carol Arnoff and her family were the Presley's neighbors on Audubon Drive. Carol often visited Elvis at his new home, and they became good friends.

1292   Dr. Metz was one of the Presleys' neighbors on Audubon Drive in Memphis.

1293   While in Las Vegas, Nevada, in April and May of 1956, Elvis was given an expensive wristwatch by an Arkansas banker. Elvis sent the man several thank you letters.

1294   By the spring of 1956, over 350,000 copies of Elvis's first album had been sold.

1295   A headline in *LIFE* magazine's April 30, 1956, issue described Elvis as "A Howling Hillbilly Success."

1296   *Newsweek* magazine featured two articles about Elvis in their May 12, 1956, issue. Their headlines read "Hillbilly on a Pedestal" and "Presley Spells Profit."

1297   Pilot Henry Cannon was called in to fly Elvis from LaCrosse, Wisconsin, to Memphis on May 12, 1956.

1298   Rising Sun, the golden palomino horse Elvis bought in 1967, was born in 1956.

1299 In the late 1950's, Elvis purchased his motorcycles from Tommy Taylor's Memphis Harley Davidson Company, located at 235 Poplar Avenue. It was owned by Benjamin W. Barfield, the company president. Vice president was Carl C. Beard and secretary/treasurer was Mrs. Louise Strickland. The company's telephone number was 5-5115.

1300 *Harley Enthusiast* magazine featured Elvis on the cover of their May 1956 issue. This was a small magazine, measuring 6" x 9," with only 23 pages.

1301 Trude Forshner was Colonel Parker's assistant in the 1950's.

1302 Elvis was interviewed by disc jockey Ray Green in Little Rock, Arkansas, on May 16, 1956.

1303 The gold record Elvis received for "Heartbreak Hotel" cost $200 to produce.

1304 In 1956, Elvis made the following comment about his rise to fame: "If anybody had told me two years ago I'd be where I am today, I'd of told him he was crazy and meant it. It's all happened so fast sometimes I can't get to sleep. It scares me you know. It scares me."

1305 Elvis reportedly gave his famous blue suede shoes to the Robinson Intermediate Fan Club from Wichita, Kansas, on May 18, 1956.

1306 In 1956, Colonel Parker was approached with an offer to have Elvis star in the Broadway production of the musical *Li'l Abner*. Parker declined.

1307 Elvis was so ashamed of buying his diamond initial ring that he did not tell his mother how much it cost.

Elvis (far right) dancing with Wink Martindale (far left) at Martindale's Dance Party show in Memphis, June 20, 1956.

1308   Three brothers owned the Hays Jewelry Store where Elvis bought much of his jewelry. Lowell Hays and his wife Dixie lived at 3280 Park Ave. Durwood E. Hays and his wife, Violet, lived at 3066 Carrington Rd. Raymond A. Hays and his wife, Edith, lived at 3398 Carrington Rd. The store was located at 801 Three Sisters Building in Memphis.

1309   In the 1950's, Elvis used a Remington Roll-A-Matic Razor Deluxe, an electric razor with a detachable cord.

1310   In 1956, Mrs. Edna Ellis fashioned girls' hair into Elvis Presley pompadours and ducktails. She pioneered the female Elvis Presley hairdo.

1311   In 1956, Elvis spent $100 at a fair, riding scooters with his friends.

1312   A student at a Rome, Michigan, high school was suspended by the principal for sporting an Elvis Presley hairstyle.

1313   Elvis's RCA-Victor records were distributed throughout the United States by McDonald Bros. The manager of the record department was Bill Graham.

1314   Leonard's Restaurant in Memphis, Tennessee, offered a special rock-n-roll menu in 1956 which featured "Don't Be Cruel Prices," "Ready Teddy Pork Chops," "Hound Dog and Sauerkraut," and "Love Me Tender Steak."

1315   Dewey Phillips collected porno tapes. When he acquired a new one, he invited Elvis over to help him decide if it was worth keeping.

1316   By 1956, Elvis Presley had become the most talked about new personality in recorded music in ten years.

1317   In 1956, Elvis wore a gold rectangular Elgin watch with a stretch band.

1318   Max H. Furbringer, owner of the firm which designed Graceland, died of a heart attack in 1956 at age 77.

1319   The Colonel helped Elvis negotiate the price of the white Lincoln Continental Elvis purchased in Florida in 1956.

1320   With the help of Sam Phillips, Bob Neal opened Stars Inc., a company that handled recording artists from the South.

1321   One in every nine records sold in 1956 was an Elvis Presley record!

1322   Elvis owned a yellow Isetta 300 car in the mid-1950's.

1323   Some time in 1956, Elvis was described by some critics as "a savage" and "a character right out of *The Blackboard Jungle*."

1324   Elvis helped to promote a "Safe Driving" campaign for teenagers in 1956.

1325   The Colonel's motto in 1956 was "Don't try to explain it, just sell it!"

1326   In 1956, Elvis established the Elvis Presley Foundation For Underprivileged Children. He donated the proceeds from several of his shows to this charity. Elvis fans from all over the world contributed funds to the foundation.

1327   When Colonel Parker hired Hank Saperstein to handle Elvis Presley merchandise, Parker demanded a $50,000 fee, the equivalent of royalties on $1 million in sales.

1328   Hank Saperstein and his partner, Howard Bell, established Specialty

Projects, Inc. Based in Beverly Hills, California, Specialty Projects handled all Elvis Presley merchandise.

1329 In 1956, Hank Saperstein was 36 years old. He was the President of Television Personalities Inc., and handled merchandise for TV shows such as *The Adventures of Wyatt Earp*, starring Hugh O'Brian; *The Lone Ranger*, starring Clayton Moore; and *Lassie*.

1330 In 1956, Elvis Presley Enterprises merchandise was aimed mainly at the female population. Elvis's fan base was, after all, 80% female!

1331 Elvis and Colonel Parker received 4-11% of the manufacturer's wholesale price on Elvis Presley products.

1332 In 1956, the very first product produced by Elvis Presley Enterprises was a glow-in-the-dark photo which sold for $1. Elvis Presley Enterprises released 100,000 copies of the photo, which was coated with a phosphorescent paint.

1333 The second product released by Elvis Presley Enterprises was lipstick. One million 1956 Elvis Presley Enterprises lipsticks were produced, in six different colors: Hound Dog Orange, Heartbreak Pink, Love-Ya Fuchsia, Tutti Frutti, Tender Pink, and Cruel Red. Manufactured by Teen-Ager Lipstick Corp. in Beverly Hills, California, each tube sold for $1.

1334 Stan Levitt of the Allison Manufacturing Company produced the 1956 Elvis Presley Enterprises Elvis T-shirt. He was supposed to make Elvis Presley pajamas as well, but never did.

1335 The Elvis Presley T-shirt came in small, medium, and large, and sold for $1.50. It was one of the most popular items made by Elvis Presley Enterprises in 1956.

1336   Elvis Presley "Go Gang Go" T-shirts sold for $1.99 in 1956.

1337   The Elvis Presley Enterprises Elvis doll sold for $3.98 in 1956.

1338   In 1956, bakeries nationwide featured Elvis Presley birthday cake decorations, licensed by Elvis Presley Enterprises.

1339   In 1956, Elvis Presley Enterprises organized a promotion called "Mr. Teenager," for which Elvis advertised various soft drinks. Elvis Presley Enterprises created 16-page booklets and colorful cardboard displays, but the promotion was scrapped.

1340   Randolph Manufacturing Company produced Elvis Presley sneakers in 1956. They came in a tan box featuring a large picture of Elvis holding a guitar on the lid and a cut-out portrait of Elvis with an autograph on the bottom. The boxes came in white with black drawings and black with white drawings.

1341   Elvis Presley Enterprises contracted with the Faith Shoe Company to manufacture Elvis Presley skimmer pumps in a variety of colors. The leather version sold for $4.99, and the fabric version sold for $3.99.

1342   Elvis Presley cuff links were manufactured in 1956, but were not sold until 1958. The gold-colored cuff links featured Elvis's name written in script with a cream-colored center.

1343   In 1956, Little Jean Togs, Inc. produced the popular Elvis Presley felt skirt.

1344   One of the rarest Elvis Presley collectibles made in 1956 was the "Elvis Paint-By-Number Set," made by Peerless Playthings Company in Richfield, New Jersey.

1345 In the late summer of 1956, an Elvis Presley Victrola sold for $32.95. It was a four-speed, portable phonograph, model 7EP2. A special RCA-Victor double-pocket EP record, *Elvis Presley* (SPD-22), was included with the Victrola.

1346 An automatic Elvis Presley 45 rpm Victrola (model 7EP45) sold for $44.95 in 1956. Included with the phonograph was an RCA-Victor triple pocket EP, *Elvis Presley* (SPD-23). This product was sold on a special easy payment plan of a dollar down and a dollar each week.

1347 A black and white Elvis Presley Photo Souvenir Package sold for 50¢ in 1956. A deluxe full-color Elvis Presley Photo Souvenir Package sold for $1.

1348 Elvis Presley Enterprises' adjustable Elvis photo rings sold for 49¢ at Woolworth's and $1 at Nordstrom's in 1956.

1349 Woolworth's sold red, white, and blue Elvis mittens for $1.50 in 1956.

1350 Leather belts made by Elvis Presley Enterprises sold for $1 in 1956. They came in small, medium, and large.

1351 1956 Elvis Presley Enterprises wallets, which came in a variety of styles, cost anywhere from 59¢ to $1.00. The wallets came in four colors: cream, brown, blue, and red.

1352 Half a million 18K gold-plated 1956 Elvis Presley Enterprises charm bracelets were sold.

1353 The Elvis Presley stationary set sold for $1 in 1956.

1354 Elvis Presley Enterprises scarves sold for $1.49 in 1956.

Elvis riding Eli at the Gulf Hills Dude Ranch & Country Club, located at 13701 Paso Road in Ocean Springs, Mississippi, June 1956.

1355 The Philadelphia Novelty Store sold two different 1956 Elvis Presley Enterprises celluloid buttons. The "I LOVE ELVIS" pin sold for 10¢ while the "I HATE ELVIS" pin sold for 15¢. Elvis Presley Enterprises even made money from people who weren't Elvis fans!

1356 There were only 150,000 Elvis Presley Enterprises Elvis statues made in 1956.

1357 The 1956 Elvis Presley Enterprises "Love Me Tender" watch with a heart locket was made by Holiday Jewelry.

1358 Seven-inch bronze statues of Elvis with a guitar were licensed by Elvis Presley Enterprises; they sold for $1.

1359 At Woolworth's, Elvis Presley polyester turban scarves sold for $1.29, while a cotton version cost $1.

1360 In 1956, an Elvis Presley "rock-n-roll" purse could be purchased for $1.

1361 Elvis Presley Enterprises novelty hats, manufactured by Irving Skolnick, came in small, medium, and large. They sold for $1 each in 1956.

1362 Elvis Presley Enterprises made pocket-sized, battery-operated Elvis Presley personal fans which cost $2.

1363 In 1956, Elvis Presley jeans sold for $2.98. They were black denim with white trim and each pair had Elvis's name embroidered on the back pocket. Two hundred thousand pairs were produced.

1364 After witnessing the impact of Elvis Presley jeans, Amalgamated Clothing Workers of America president Jacob Potofsky stated that teenagers were more likely to listen to Elvis than to their teachers.

1365   A pair of Elvis Presley socks sold for $1 in 1956.

1366   Some of the Elvis Presley Enterprises products sold in 5 & 10 stores nationwide in 1956 included bobby socks, combs, brushes, pillows, toy guitars, cologne, Plaster of Paris busts, jewelry, pencils, celluloid buttons, and banners.

1367   It was reported that an Elvis Presley soft drink was created in 1956.

1368   Over 78 Elvis Presley Enterprises products were manufactured in 1956.

1369   It was reported that sales of Elvis Presley Enterprises products were greater than sales of Davy Crockett products in 1956.

1370   An Elvis Presley candy was produced in 1956. Called the Elvis Presley Teddy Bear Candy Bar, it consisted of milk chocolate, puffed wheat, crushed almonds, and Brazil nuts. It had a silver and black wrapper, was about the size of a Baby Ruth candy bar, and was sold in movie theaters.

1371   Some of the Elvis Presley Enterprises items that were reportedly sold in 1956 included hair curlers, wolf whistles, Bermuda shorts, and dog food.

1372   In 1956, Hank Saperstein wanted to make Elvis Presley Ivy League shirts and pants for girls, but that never happened.

1373   Elvis Presley products were sold in the following stores throughout the United States in 1956: Sears & Roebuck, Montgomery Ward, W.T. Grant, Woolworth's, AMC Stores, Macy's, Allied Department Stores, H.L. Green, Rexall, and Whelan Drug Stores.

1374 All purchases of Elvis Presley Enterprises merchandise had to be paid for in cash and were non-returnable.

1375 Howard Bell was the manufacturer of 1956 Elvis Presley Enterprises merchandise for Special Products, Inc.

1376 The first Elvis Presley sheet music by RCA-Victor was "Mystery Train."

1377 In 1956, sheet music for "Hound Dog" came in two versions: the one for guitar was printed in blue and the one for piano was printed in brown.

1378 A magazine once called Elvis "The Tune Tornado."

1379 Gladys Presley felt that Colonel Parker treated Elvis like a product rather than a person. She did not trust him.

1380 In 1956, Elvis bought his mother a deep fryer to use when making her famous fried chicken.

1381 In 1956, Elvis traded his Lincoln for a white Lincoln Continental Mark II at Schilling Motors, located at 987 Union Avenue in Memphis. The hood ornament on the car cost $350.

1382 In the 1950's, thousands of girls sent Elvis their high school rings along with love-filled letters asking him to wear the rings around his neck and be their boyfriend. The rings were mailed back to their owners.

1383 In the middle to late 1950's, several reporters referred to Colonel Parker as "Elvis's seeing-eye manager."

1384 Elvis used pancake makeup, mascara, and eye shadow while touring in the middle to late 1950's. The pancake makeup was used to hide his acne.

1385 In the 1950's, the Brinkley Distribution Company in Jacksonville, Florida, initially ordered 50 copies of each Elvis 78 rpm record and 100 of each Elvis 45 rpm record.

1386 In an interview in the mid-1950's, the Colonel had this to say about Elvis: "I'm going to get a "wiggle-eter" to time the wiggles. When Elvis stops singing, he'll wiggle!"

1387 Sometime in 1956, Elvis carried a .22-caliber gun while touring.

1388 In 1956, Elvis owned forty suits and forty-five sport shirts.

1389 In 1956, Elvis stated that he had a bad habit of leaving the engines of his cars running when he parked.

1390 Elvis bought gas for his cars and motorcycles at Vicker's Gas Station in Memphis.

1391 The magazine *Elvis Speaks* was published by Rave Publishing Company in 1956. It featured a cardboard record called *The Truth About Me*, which was produced by Rainbo Records in Lawndale, California. The initial print run for the magazine was 300,000 copies.

1392 In 1956, Elvis purchased a light lavender shirt with a black ribbon threaded through the collar for $70.

1393 In 1956, it was rumored that Elvis had leukemia. Colonel Parker set the record straight immediately.

1394 Elvis was a big fan of Barq's Root Beer in 1956. Since the soda was only available on the Mississippi coast, he ordered several cases and had them shipped to Memphis.

1395 To relax after their strenuous touring schedule, Elvis and his entourage visited the Gulf Hills Dude Ranch & Country Club at 13701 Paso Road in Ocean Springs, Mississippi.

1396 While at Gulf Hills, Elvis enjoyed horseback riding. The horse he rode was named Eli.

1397 Elvis and Charley Voivedich used BB guns to target shoot at the Gulf Hills Country Club in Mississippi in June of 1956. Some of the items they shot at were 45 rpm records, matchsticks, and candles.

1398 Elvis rented a house from the Hack family while visiting the Gulf Hills Country Club in Ocean Springs, Mississippi, in 1956.

1399 Elvis ate at Gus Stevens' Restaurant in Biloxi, Mississippi, while vacationing at the Gulf Hills Dude Ranch & Country Club.

1400 When Elvis's family joined him in Biloxi, they stayed at the Surf and Sand Hotel.

1401 Elvis made a special appearance at a shoe store in downtown Biloxi in August of 1956. Over 100 fans jammed into the small store, which was owned by Lew Sonnier.

1402 In 1956, Memphis diners served special platters with hot-dogs called "Hound Dogs" and hamburgers called "Hound Burgers." The platters sold for 89-98¢.

1403 In 1956, ice cream parlors, candy stores, and soda shops across the United States were allowed to call themselves "Elvis Centers" for a small franchise fee of $2 per week, to be paid to Elvis Presley

Elvis wearing the unfamiliar and constricting tux and tails on The Steve Allen Show, *July 1, 1956. Here Allen is discussing the skit with a rigid and rather humiliated Elvis.*

Enterprises. Approximately 48,000 establishments took part. These "Elvis Centers" franchises were rumored to be run by "Operation Snotnose."

1404 Elvis enjoyed reading *Playboy* magazine.

1405 Colonel Parker boiled most of his dinners, as he did when he worked with the circuses. He also loved barbecue.

1406 In 1956, Colonel Parker carried a cane because he had a bad back. He wore a back brace from his waist to his upper back.

1407 Because the Colonel was always chomping on cigars, he began talking from the side of his mouth.

1408 A disc jockey from California sponsored a national "Be Kind to Elvis" day in 1956. He played Elvis's music for 24 hours straight!

1409 CJCH Radio in Halifax, Nova Scotia, banned all Elvis records in 1956.

1410 In 1956, *16* magazine sponsored a contest called "Why I Think Elvis is the Greatest Star of All." Prizes included a 1956 Elvis Presley Enterprises charm bracelet, a framed portrait of Elvis, Elvis perfume, an Elvis photo album, an Elvis scrapbook, 3 autographed photos, copies of all of Elvis's LP records, a Teen Queen wallet with Elvis's and the winner's initials on it, an engraved and autographed Elvis photo, an Elvis Presley T-shirt, and a subscription to *16* magazine.

1411 Elvis's favorite water skiing spot was McKellar Lake, located at Treasure Island on an old channel bed of the Mississippi River. The lake was named after Senator Kenneth McKellar.

1412 In 1956, Elvis went water skiing at McKellar Lake with Charles "Sonny" Neal (Bob Neal's son), instructor Dickie Waters, and Jim Chaffman, who usually operated the speedboat.

1413 Elvis wore checked swimming trunks when he went water skiing in the 1950's.

1414 In the 1950's, Elvis liked to eat half a cantaloupe with a scoop of vanilla ice cream for breakfast.

1415 In the 1950's, the sight of a stuffed lobster or red, bloody meat sickened Elvis.

1416 In 1956, the first Elvis Presley National Fan Club offered its members three kits. The first included a song folio, an 11 x 14 color portrait, an 8 x 10 pink autographed photo, and an "I LIKE ELVIS AND HIS RCA RECORDS" button. It cost $1. The second kit consisted of the 8 x 10 photo, a 5 x 7 face photo, and the button. It cost 50¢. The third kit included the 5 x 7 photo, the button, and a wallet-sized photo. It cost 25¢.

1417 The Lansky brothers, owners of Lansky's Clothing Emporium in Memphis where Elvis shopped, opened seven stores within the state of Tennessee. Five of them were called "Hercules-Big Men" stores.

1418 Sandra McCune, President of the Oakland Elvis Presley Fan Club, met Elvis in 1956. Elvis got a kick out of the fact that she wore an Elvis Presley Enterprises T-shirt to their meeting.

1419 Elvis's cousin, Gene Smith, was drafted into the US Army in 1956.

1420 Fans broke into Elvis's Cadillac one day in 1956 and stole his cigarette lighter collection.

1421 In 1956, one of the oldest Elvis fans was Mrs. P.E. Mitchell, an 80-year-old woman from Memphis.

1422 The famous Top 40 list was "born" at the same time Elvis's songs hit the world.

1423 Record player companies saw an increase in business thanks to Elvis's popularity.

1424 Elvis's favorite flower was jasmine.

1425 In 1956, a critic had this to say about Elvis: "Is it a sausage? It is certainly smooth and damp looking, but who ever heard of a 172 pound sausage, 6 foot tall?"

1426 In 1956, Mrs. Bernard (Joyce) Lansky, wife of one of the owners of Lansky's Clothing Emporium, said, "They talk about juvenile delinquency. Here's a boy who didn't have much except what was in himself, and I think he has done a pretty good job of lifting himself. Give the boy a break!"

1427 One fan loved Elvis so much that she carved his name into her arm four times!

1428 With Elvis's help, Gladys had her own savings account which allowed her to spend her own money as she pleased.

1429 It was rumored that a man broke one of Elvis's records over Colonel Parker's head in 1956.

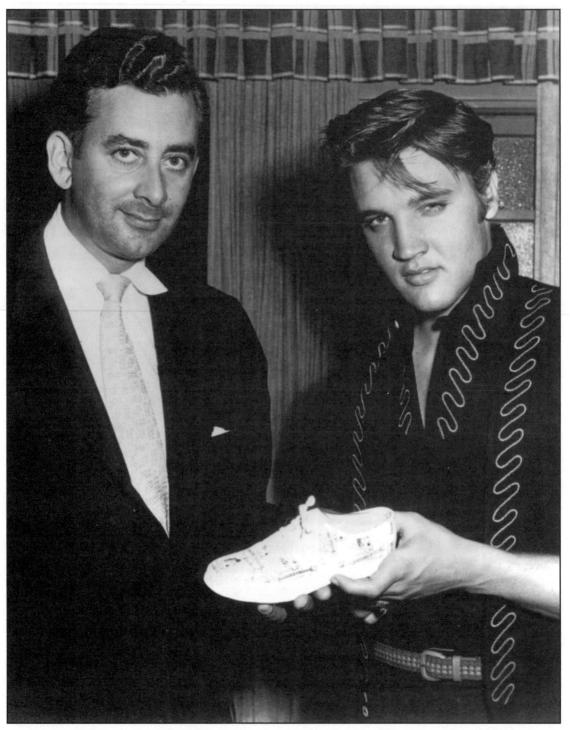

Elvis with Hank Saperstein, the man who turned "Elvis Presley" into a household name, late summer 1956. Saperstein marketed Elvis Presley merchandise, which made millions.

1430 Elvis was interviewed by Lou Irwin after his Shrine Auditorium show in Los Angeles, California, on June 8, 1956.

1431 The Colonel designed every one of Elvis's RCA-Victor album covers.

1432 Around 1956, it was reported that Elvis was allergic to iodine.

1433 Elvis appeared on *The Milton Berle Show* for the second time on June 5, 1956.

1434 Elvis's second *Milton Berle* appearance on June 5, 1956, was filmed in and broadcast from Burbank, California.

1435 Elvis sang "Hound Dog" and "I Want You, I Need You, I Love You" during his second performance on *The Milton Berle Show*.

1436 Elvis first used the Jordanaires as his backup group during his June 5th, 1956, appearance on *The Milton Berle Show*.

1437 After Elvis finished singing "Hound Dog" on *The Milton Berle Show* in June of 1956, Milton came out and did a little dance, Elvis-style.

1438 Elvis received $5,000 for his second appearance on *The Milton Berle Show*.

1439 *The Milton Berle Show* was broadcast in the United States in color. When it was released on video tape, however, the program was in black and white.

1440 The June 5, 1956, episode of *The Milton Berle Show* was sponsored by RCA-Victor and was Milton Berle's last show.

1441 Elvis was harassed about wiggling on *The Milton Berle Show* on June 5, 1956, and his response was: "Did you see that show? This Debra Paget is on the same show. She wore a tight thing with feathers on the behind where they wiggle the most. And I never saw anything like it! Sex? Man, she bumped and pooshed out all over the place. I'm like Little Boy Blue and who do they say is obscene? ME! It's because I make more money than Debra. Them critics don't like to see nobody win, doing any kind of music they don't know nothin' about!"

1442 By mid-1956, the handling of Elvis's career at RCA-Victor had been handed over to Anne Fulchino, publicist of the Pop Record division.

1443 In June of 1956, RCA publicist Anne Fulchino hired photographer Alfred Wertheimer to follow Elvis for a few weeks. He was ordered to take black and white photos only; RCA-Victor did not want to spend the extra money for color film because they still believed that the Elvis craze would die out in six months.

1444 Alfred Wertheimer took a train ride with Elvis from New York City to Memphis. He took photos of Elvis sleeping, reading, listening to records, getting dressed, shaving, combing his hair, and performing on *The Steve Allen Show*.

1445 Elvis enjoyed reading *Archie*, *Jughead*, and *Veronica* comic books when traveling by train in the 1950's.

1446 On June 20, 1956, Elvis made a brief appearance on *Wink Martindale's Dance Party*. The program was broadcast on KLAC-TV in Memphis.

1447 On Dance Party, Elvis was asked if, in high school, he had expected to become so famous. He replied, "I never expected to get out of Humes High School."

1448 On June 27, 1956, it was announced that Elvis was responsible for over 20% of RCA-Victor's single record sales.

1449 The Gibson Guitar Corp. presented Elvis with a 1956 guitar as a gift of thanks for publicizing their company. Gibson was the make of guitar Elvis preferred.

1450 To get to New York City for a television appearance and recording session, Elvis took a train from Central Station at South Main and Calhoun Streets in Memphis. He arrived in New York on June 29, 1956.

1451 Rehearsals for *The Steve Allen Show* were held on Friday morning, June 29, 1956. Elvis was the first person to arrive at the Hudson Theater for rehearsal.

1452 *The Steve Allen Show* was broadcast from the Hudson Theater, located at 145 W. 44th Street in New York City. The Hudson, opened in 1903, was the second oldest Broadway theater in the city.

1453 Elvis first appeared on *The Steve Allen Show* on July 1, 1956.

1454 Steve Allen's secretary, Doris Braverman, handled all of the paperwork regarding Elvis's appearance on *The Steve Allen Show*.

1455 After rehearsals for *The Steve Allen Show*, Elvis was informed that the tailor had arrived and was ready to meet with him. When Elvis asked what for, Steve Allen told him that his performance required him to wear a tuxedo and sing to a basset hound!

1456 Milton Berle went backstage at *The Steve Allen Show* to wish Elvis luck.

1457 On his show, Steve Allen introduced Elvis by saying, "It gives me great pleasure to introduce the new Elvis Presley." Elvis then came on stage wearing a tuxedo.

1458 Elvis sang "Hound Dog" to Sherlock, a tuxedo-clad basset hound on *The Steve Allen Show*. He also sang "I Want You, I Need You, I Love You."

1459 Steve Allen's orchestra conductor was Skitch Henderson.

1460 A giant roll of paper—a collection of 18,000 signatures asking that Elvis appear on *The Steve Allen Show*—was brought on stage during the show by Gene Rayburn. Steve Allen said that the list had been sent by disc jockey Don Williams from Tulsa, Oklahoma.

1461 On *The Steve Allen Show* in 1956, Elvis participated in a comedy skit called "Range Roundup." In it, he played "Tumbleweed Presley" and performed a commercial spoof for the fictitious "Tonto Candy Bar." "Tumbleweed Presley's" lines were sung: "I've gotta horse—I've gotta gun. I'm going out and have me some fun. But I'm warning you Galoots, Don't you step on my blue suede boots!"

1462 Elvis was paid $5,000 for each appearance on *The Steve Allen Show*.

1463 Elvis was contacted by Ed Sullivan backstage at *The Steve Allen Show* in 1956. When asked if he would appear on *The Ed Sullivan Show*, Elvis explained that he could not negotiate a deal without Colonel Parker present.

1464 The July 1, 1956, episode of *The Steve Allen Show* featuring Elvis received a 20.2 Trendex rating and a 55.3% share of the audience.

1465 Elvis was interviewed by phone by Hy Gardner after his appearance on *The Steve Allen Show* in 1956. Camera crews filmed both Elvis and Gardner, and the interview was shown on TV with a split-screen.

1466 Elvis's interview for *Hy Gardner Calling* took place at 11:30 p.m., July 1, 1956, at the Warwick Hotel. Gardner was at the WRCA-TV Channel 4 studio. The interview aired the following evening.

1467 On July 2, 1956, Elvis had his final recording session in RCA's New York studio. He recorded "Hound Dog," "Don't Be Cruel," and "Any Way You Want Me."

1468 The Jordanaires were used for the second time during Elvis's July 2, 1956, recording session.

1469 Alfred Wertheimer took photographs of Elvis during his final recording session in RCA's New York studio.

1470 During the final RCA New York recording session, Elvis's lunch consisted of a turkey sandwich on rye bread, chicken salad, a slice of apple pie, and a Pepsi.

1471 After his appearance on *The Steve Allen Show*, Elvis took a train home from New York to Memphis. He left New York on Tuesday, July 3, 1956, at 11:30 a.m.

1472 The train Elvis took home from New York in July of 1956 arrived in Memphis and stopped at Poplar Avenue between Colonial and Mendenhall Roads. As there was no station, Elvis was simply let off. Twenty-eight hours after his departure from New York, he arrived back home.

Elvis in court, standing in front of the judge, with Jim Aubrey and Edd Hopper standing to his right, October 19, 1956. The judge sided with Elvis in the infamous gas station fight.

1473 RCA-Victor released a 45 rpm record of "Hound Dog"/"Don't Be Cruel" in July of 1956.

1474 On July 4, 1956, at the Russwood Park located at 914 Madison Avenue in Memphis, Elvis donated his famous $600, 14-diamond initial ring to be raffled off as a door prize.

1475 Seventeen-year-old Roger Fakes was the lucky winner of Elvis's ring, raffled off on the Fourth of July in 1956. The winning number was 9736.

1476 On July 4, 1956, five teenagers were arrested at a beer party in Ottawa, Canada. One of the teenagers who pleaded guilty to underage drinking was the president of an Elvis Presley Fan Club.

1477 On July 16, 1956, *Newsweek* printed a story relating to Elvis's appearance in a tuxedo on *The Steve Allen Show*. The article read, "Allen dressed Elvis like a corpse!"

1478 The July 21, 1956, issue of England's *Melody Maker* magazine featured an article written by T. Brown entitled "Elvis Presley" that suggested to readers that they should not buy Elvis's records.

1479 The license plate of Elvis's 1956 ivory-colored Cadillac El Dorado convertible was 8J-3003 (Tennessee).

1480 In the 1950's, Elvis rarely used the air conditioning in his cars. He preferred rolling down the windows instead.

1481 *American Bandstand* honored Elvis with an "Elvis Day" in 1956 for being the "Teenage Champion of the Year." Elvis was the first entertainer to earn this honor.

1482 Elvis read *DIG* magazine in the 1950's. He especially enjoyed reading the articles about himself.

1483 In 1956, Gladys Presley had this to say about her son's fans: "I greet them all with respect and entertain them real nice! Many want to dance to Elvis's records, so I put them on and let them. Some want souvenirs, bricks from the house, clovers from the lawn."

1484 Elvis's fans often tore down the hedges and dug up dirt from his Audubon Drive house in Memphis to package and sell as souvenirs.

1485 In mid-1956, one of Elvis's Audubon Drive neighbors was quoted as saying, "We've had to call the police time after time to get those screeching female adolescents to go away. I don't like to be thought a snob, but frankly the Presleys don't belong here. I wish they'd move. Why, one family just had to go away to Florida to get some rest!"

1486 In 1956, Mrs. Frank Jemison, one of the Presleys' neighbors on Audubon Drive in Memphis, said, "We had a nice quiet street, but now we get more traffic than downtown Main Street. And the kids, sometimes hundreds at a time, just hang around his front yard, climb the fence, rap on the windows, to try to get Elvis to look out. Now I'm not saying that's the Presleys' fault, mind you. They're fine as neighbors, nice as can be. Why, I even went over to get an autograph for a friend myself and Elvis gave my daughter one of his stuffed animals!"

1487 Elvis had a large cage set up in his Audubon Drive home for his monkeys, Jayhew and Jimbo. It was the size of half a room and came complete with trapezes.

1488 Many unflattering nicknames were bestowed upon Elvis during the early part of his career, including "The Great Gyrator" and "Pulsating

Presley." Other nicknames in the 1950's included "The Hillbilly Cat," "Elvis the Pelvis," "The King of Western Bop," "The Memphis Flash," "Sir Swivel Hips," and "The Atomic Powered Singer."

1489   Elvis met Charlie Hodge for the first time in 1956. Charlie was a member of the Foggy River Boys, a gospel quartet.

1490   In mid-July of 1956, the Colonel made a deal with Ed Sullivan to have Elvis appear on Sullivan's television show.

1491   Gladys and Vernon collected everything published about Elvis. The scrapbooks they created included hundreds of newspaper articles, magazine stories, and photographs.

1492   Elvis kept his own scrapbook of clippings about himself—but he only included articles with positive things to say about him.

1493   On August 1, 1956, Elvis was ticketed for speeding in Hattiesburg, Mississippi, by Constable Charlie Ward.

1494   In 1956, the license plate of Elvis's white Cadillac was 2D-33501 (Tennessee).

1495   On August 3, 1956, Elvis was interviewed by a panel of reporters from the *Miami Herald*.

1496   Elvis purchased a new Lincoln convertible in Miami, Florida, on August 3, 1956.

1497   The license plate on Elvis's new white Lincoln was 2D-33503 (Tennessee).

1498   *The Miami Daily News* called Elvis "The Squirmer" in their August 4, 1956, issue.

1499   The August 1956 issue of *Look* magazine included an article entitled, "Elvis Presley, He Can't Be, But He Is."

1500   August 6, 1956, marked the date of one of the most important interviews of Elvis's budding career: reporter Paul Wilder interviewed Elvis in Lakeland, Florida, for *TV Guide*.

1501   Elvis wore black pants, a baby blue silk shirt, and white buck shoes for his *TV Guide* interview in 1956.

1502   Colonel Parker was interviewed for *TV Guide* at the same time Elvis was in 1956. He told Paul Wilder that Elvis owned 25-30 stage suits.

1503   The *TV Guide* article from 1956 was entitled "The Plain Truth About Elvis Presley."

1504   Anne Rowe, the twenty-one year old editor of the "Teen Time Turntable" weekly column in the *St. Petersburg Florida Times*, interviewed Elvis after his show at the Florida Theater on August 7, 1956.

1505   The August 8, 1956, issue of the *Evening Independent* newspaper from St. Petersburg, Florida, featured a photo of Elvis on the front cover along with the headline, "Elvis is the Pied Piper of Rock-n-Roll."

1506   In August of 1956, two columnists from the *Vancouver Sun* ran contests at the same time on the same page of the newspaper. Jack Scott ran a "WHY I LIKE ELVIS PRESLEY" contest with movie tickets as prizes, while Jack Wasserman ran a "WHY I HATE ELVIS PRESLEY" contest with Frank Sinatra records as prizes.

1507 Elvis received a vote for President against Dwight D. Eisenhower in 1956. The vote came from Lowndes County, Mississippi.

1508 The first ever color pin-up of Elvis appeared in the August 1956 issue of *Modern Screen* magazine. Debbie Reynolds adorned the cover.

1509 Elvis spent $700 at the Long Beach Amusement Park on a Saturday night in August of 1956.

1510 In 1956, Elvis was called a "male burlesque queen."

1511 On August 30, 1956, Elvis received a death threat via postcard. It read, "If you don't stop this shit, we're going to kill you!" It was postmarked Niagara Falls, New York. The FBI was notified of the death threat, and they created a special file for Elvis, number 9-30861-1.

1512 John Crosby, a 1950's syndicated TV critic from New York, called Elvis "A shouter... who yells a song and seems to have some sort of St. Vitus dance... a candidate for a spastic hospital."

1513 Elvis was forced to work on Labor Day in 1956. He recorded thirteen songs in Studio B of Radio Recorders in Hollywood, California, from September 1-3.

1514 When Elvis recorded at Radio Recorders, he carried press clippings about himself and showed them to everyone.

1515 On September 1, 1956, Elvis recorded "Playing For Keeps," "Love Me," "How Do You Think I Feel," and "How's The World Treating You."

1516 On September 2, 1956, Elvis recorded "Paralyzed," "When My Blue

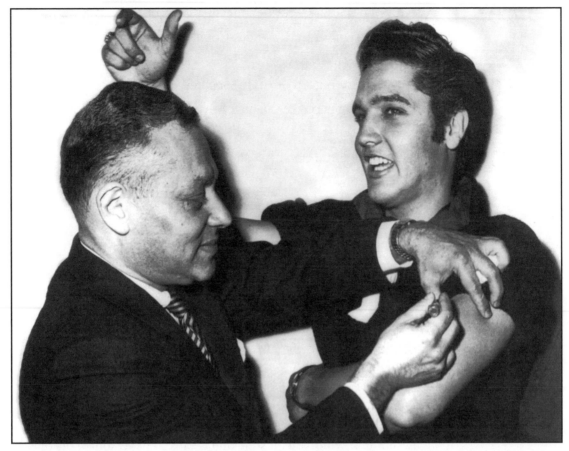

Elvis receiving a polio shot from Dr. Harold T. Furst of the New York Department of Health, October 28, 1956.

Moon Turns to Gold Again," "Long Tall Sally," "Old Shep," "Too Much," and "Anyplace Is Paradise."

1517 On September 3, 1956, Elvis recorded "Ready Teddy," "First in Line," and "Rip It Up."

1518 Elvis did not like the taste of butter and chose to eat margarine instead. He thought that butter tasted stale.

1519 Whenever Elvis was home, Gladys made him grits for breakfast.

1520 Elvis bought his mother her famous pink Fleetwood Cadillac on September 3, 1956, from Southern Motors, located at 341 Union Avenue in Memphis. The Cadillac was originally baby blue in color and was repainted pink.

1521 One of Elvis's fans stole the hubcaps off Gladys's pink Cadillac in 1956—while the vehicle was parked in the Presleys' Audubon Drive carport!

1522 In addition to the pink Cadillac, Elvis also purchased a white 1956 Cadillac El Dorado from Southern Motors on Union Avenue in Memphis. In later years the car was restored and painted purple.

1523 RCA-Victor released seven Elvis Presley singles at the same time in 1956. Each 45 rpm record sold 100,000 copies. Elvis received a 7¢ royalty per record, earning him a total of $49,000! These were the only singles released by RCA-Victor without a picture sleeve.

1524 The TV Guide interview with Elvis ran in their September 8, 1956, issue. A close-up of Elvis's face while singing was displayed on the cover.

1525 A limited edition 45 rpm record, made from edited highlights of the *TV Guide* interview from 1956 and including a special message from Elvis, was distributed to disc jockeys nationwide. Only 500 copies were made; today these records are worth $5,000 each.

1526 Out of all the names Elvis was called in the 1950's, the one he hated most was "Elvis the Pelvis." He said it was "the most childish expression coming from an adult."

1527 Elvis conducted a press conference with Ed Sullivan several hours before his September 9, 1956, appearance on *The Ed Sullivan Show*. Colonel Parker wore an Elvis Presley Enterprises 1956 T-shirt under his blazer for the event.

1528 Although the September 9, 1956, *Sullivan* show was broadcast from CBS Studio 50 at 1697 Broadway in New York, Elvis did his segment from CBS Television Studio in Studio 33, located at 7800 Beverly Boulevard in Los Angeles.

1529 When Elvis made his first appearance on *The Ed Sullivan Show*, over 26,000 people requested tickets. Unfortunately, only 728 seats were available!

1530 Minutes before his first appearance on *The Ed Sullivan Show*, Elvis had his hair trimmed by Robert Keats.

1531 Ed Sullivan was in a car accident in Seymour, Connecticut, on August 6, 1956. As he was in the hospital at the time of Elvis's appearance on his show, he had actor Charles Laughton serve as host in his place.

1532 For Elvis's September 9, 1956, appearance on *The Ed Sullivan Show*, the sound crew set up microphones near Elvis's and the Blue Moon

Boys' amplifiers so that the television listening audience could hear over the screaming fans in the studio audience as Elvis sang "Don't Be Cruel," "Love Me Tender," "Ready Teddy," and "Hound Dog."

1533 Gordon Stoker of the Jordanaires backed Elvis on the piano during his performance of "Ready Teddy" during Elvis's Sullivan Show appearance on September 9, 1956.

1534 Ed Sullivan's orchestra conductor was Ray Bloch.

1535 *The Ed Sullivan Show* was sponsored by Lincoln-Mercury.

1536 Elvis wore clothes from Lansky's during his first appearance on *The Ed Sullivan Show*.

1537 In September of 1956, the highest paid performer to date on *The Ed Sullivan Show* had been Sonja Henie, who received $13,000 for her appearance. When Elvis arrived on the scene, however, he broke the record with an unheard of $17,000 for his appearance!

1538 Scotty Moore, Bill Black, and DJ Fontana each received $78.23 for their *The Ed Sullivan Show* appearances.

1539 *The Ed Sullivan Show* received an 82.6% share of the viewing audience when Elvis made his first appearance.

1540 Elvis visited Catalina Island after his performance on *The Ed Sullivan Show* on September 9, 1956.

1541 In September of 1956, Gladys stated that the Presleys were receiving over 1,000 letters per week. Half of those were complaints from parents to Gladys and Vernon!

1542 The *Elvis Presley* EP (EPA-830) was released by RCA-Victor in September of 1956.

1543 The *Real Elvis* EP (EPA-940) was released by RCA-Victor in September of 1956.

1544 Elvis bought his mother a miniature Pomeranian in 1956. "Sweetpea" quickly became Gladys's favorite pet; she constantly hugged and kissed him.

1545 In 1956, Elvis bought his grandfather, Jessie D. Pressley, a car and a television set. He personally delivered the gifts to Jessie at his home in Kentucky.

1546 In September of 1956, *Coronet* magazine published an article entitled "Craze Called Elvis," written by C. Brown.

1547 On October 3, 1956, Elvis's L.C. Humes High School teacher, Mildred Scrivener, appeared on a game show called *Twenty-One* in New York. She lost to a writer from Oneonta, New York. When host Jack Benny asked Mildred about Elvis Presley, she mentioned that she knew him and that he had been a student of hers.

1548 Sometime in 1956, Elvis was given a captain's badge from the Louisiana Highway Patrol. Thus began Elvis's passion for collecting badges and law enforcement credentials.

1549 On October 10, 1956, the Baker Electronic Company filed a lien for $340.62 against Elvis and the contractors who built the swimming pool at his 1034 Audubon Drive house in Memphis. It is not known if Elvis ever paid that lien.

1550   In 1956, Elvis was sued by a girl he knew named Roberta Moore for eating her sandwich and drinking her milk at a diner in Memphis. Moore sued for $42,500 but was paid $5,500 after a settlement was reached.

1551   *Variety* magazine's October 10, 1956, headline read, "Disks Jump Presley Groove."

1552   On September 30, 1956, in a public statement referencing Elvis and Rock-n-Roll music, Cardinal Spellman of Buffalo, New York, said, "A new creed has been patterned by a segment of the young people in America... a creed of dishonesty, violence, lust, and degeneration."

1553   The first radio "station break" Elvis recorded was on October 11, 1956, in Dallas, Texas. The spot was for Don Keyes of KTSA Radio in San Antonio, Texas.

1554   On October 8, 1956, Elvis turned down NBC's request to have him sing in a Kraft Television Theater segment titled "The Singing Idol," which was based on Elvis. When the Colonel quoted NBC a price of $300,000, they withdrew their request. The show aired without Elvis's voice on January 30, 1957.

1555   Elvis was interviewed by Al Hickock of KEYS Radio in Corpus Christi, Texas, on October 13, 1956.

1556   A San Francisco newspaper printed a story on Elvis entitled, "What Makes Elvis Roll On? Story of a Jelly-Kneed Kid Galahad," in their October 15, 1956, issue.

1557   The October 17, 1956, issue of *Variety* magazine included a story entitled, "Baptist Minister's Sermon vs. Elvis: He'll Hit the Skids."

Elvis and Hungerford Furniture Company representative Bill Carrier, Jr., holding a drawer from a mahogany bureau, December 1956. This was Elvis's second commericial. The ad was never used.

1558 At 5:00 p.m. on October 18, 1956, Elvis had an altercation with two gas station attendants, Aubrey Brown and Edd Hopper, at the Gulf station located on Second Street and Gayoso Avenue in Memphis.

1559 After news of Elvis's October 1956 fight at a Memphis gas station got out, Elvis was offered $10,000 by Chicago promoter Fred Kohler to referee a wrestling match. Elvis declined.

1560 Elvis enjoyed amusement parks and frequented the Mid-South Fairgrounds Amusement Park in the 1950's. The fairgrounds were located at 940 Early Maxwell Blvd. in Memphis.

1561 Elvis's favorite ride at the fairgrounds was the Zippin' Pippin' rollercoaster. Each ride on the wooden coaster cost 50¢, and Elvis was known to ride it 15 to 20 times in a row!

1562 Elvis's second album, *Elvis* (LPM-1382), was released on October 19, 1956.

1563 On October 19, 1956, RCA-Victor released the EP *Elvis, Vol. 1* (EPA-992).

1564 In the 1950's, Elvis fans often wrote threatening letters to disc jockeys, demanding that his music be played on the radio.

1565 Elvis and Dewey Phillips frequented the State Cafe, located at 84 Beale Street. Elvis lost two of his expensive porcelain tooth caps there in 1956. One was stepped on by a patron.

1566 In 1956, there was a girl living in Hopkins, Tennessee, named Elva Parsley!

1567 In 1956, the Colonel was quoted as saying, "Elvis doesn't rock-n-roll. When teenagers listen to him, they sit in their seats and soon begin to jump. And that's what his music should be called— 'sit-n-jump!'"

1568 Many people swear that Elvis owned a pink Harley Davidson motorcycle in 1956.

1569 It is true that Elvis owned a 1956 black and orange K model Harley Davidson motorcycle. The license plate on Elvis's motorcycle was 2-447 (Tennessee).

1570 Elvis was made an honorary captain of the Louisiana State Highway Patrol in the fall of 1956.

1571 *Variety* magazine bestowed the title of "The King of Rock-n-Roll" on Elvis on October 24, 1956.

1572 An October 1956 front page headline of *Variety* magazine read, "Elvis a Millionaire in One Year!"

1573 RCA-Victor released a special EP, *Perfect For Parties* (SPA-7-37) on October 25, 1956. On the album, Elvis introduces five song by various artists, as well as performs "Love Me."

1574 Elvis first dyed his hair black in late October of 1956.

1575 Elvis stopped using makeup and began to dye his eyebrows and eyelashes at the same time be began dying his hair.

1576 On October 28, 1956, Dr. Harold T. Furst (b. April 15, 1913) of the New York City Department of Health gave Elvis a very public vaccination for polio. Photos of Elvis receiving the shot appeared in newspapers throughout the country, including *The New York Times*, the day following the event.

1577 New York City Health Commissioner Dr. Leona Baumbartner urged everyone under 40 to get vaccinated "just like Elvis" in October of 1956.

1578 In 1956, RCA-Victor released a special promotional 16-inch transcription record of Elvis promoting the March of Dimes. It was distributed exclusively to radio stations.

1579 On October 28, 1956, Elvis made his second appearance on *The Ed Sullivan Show*. The program was taped at the Maxine Theater, located on 39th Street in New York City.

1580 Taping of the October 28th episode of *The Ed Sullivan Show* on which Elvis made his second appearance was delayed a few hours because of snow.

1581 During Elvis's second appearance on *The Ed Sullivan Show*, he sang "Don't Be Cruel," "Love Me Tender," "Love Me," and "Hound Dog."

1582 Elvis bungled the words to the song "Love Me" during his performance on *The Ed Sullivan Show* on October 28, 1956. Instead of singing "I will beg and steal" he sang "I need somebody" while stuttering badly.

1583 A girl from Chicago won a trip to New York City to attend the October 28th *The Ed Sullivan Show* and to meet Elvis.

1584 Someone wrote "Elvis Presley Go Home!" in chalk on the sidewalk near the Maxine Theater where Elvis taped *The Ed Sullivan Show* in October of 1956.

Elvis with the famous gospel quartet The Jordanaires, December 1956. Pictured are Gordon Stoker (first tenor), Neal Matthews (second tenor), Hoyt Hawkins (baritone), and Hugh Jarrett (bass).

1585   Gordon Sinclair interviewed Elvis on October 28, 1956, in New York City. When asked what his nationality was, Elvis replied, "Irish-American."

1586   Gladys Presley was treated for a nervous condition some time in late 1956.

1587   *Cash Box* magazine's "Best Vocalist of 1956" list: Best Male Vocalist: #1) Elvis Presley with 64,927 votes; Best R&B Vocalist: #6) Elvis Presley with 25,687 votes; Best Country Male Vocalist: #1) Elvis Presley with 54,127 votes.

1588   *Cash Box* magazine's "Best Record of 1956" list: #1) "Don't Be Cruel," with 63,928 votes; #6) "Heartbreak Hotel," with 50,317 votes; #16) "I Want You, I Need You, I Love You," with 32,672 votes; #27) "Love Me Tender," with 19,550 votes.

1589   *Cash Box* magazine's "Best R&B Record of 1956" list: #16) "Don't Be Cruel," with 14,873 votes; #22) "Heartbreak Hotel," with 12,061 votes.

1590   *Cash Box* magazine's "Best Country Record of 1956" list: #2) "Don't Be Cruel," with 50,063 votes; #4) "Heartbreak Hotel," with 43,512 votes; #8) "Hound Dog," with 29,465 votes; #10) "Love Me Tender," with 24,840 votes; #15) "I Want You, I Need You, I Love You," with 17,732 votes.

1591   In October of 1956, 16-year-old Robert Phernetton was expelled from school in Romeo, Michigan, for having an Elvis Presley haircut!

1592   On November 1, 1956, Elvis insured his Lincoln Continental Mark II with Assigned Risk Insurance Company, located at 1666 Madison Avenue in Memphis.

1593 Elvis's car registration for his Lincoln Mark II was 2D-35184.

1594 Al Hickock interviewed Elvis for the second time on November 2, 1956, in San Antonio, Texas.

1595 In November of 1956, Elvis recorded a radio commercial to promote RCA-Victor's new Elvis Presley record players.

1596 RCA-Victor released the *Elvis, Vol. 2* EP (EPA-933) in November of 1956.

1597 In November of 1956, Reverend Edward J. Hales of New Bedford, Massachusetts, had this to say about Elvis: "Elvis will be less popular in a year or two. I feel that the emotional nature of young people has produced Elvis Presley. Part of adolescence is change. We are living in a world where it's pretty hard for even adults to remain emotionally stable."

1598 On November 6, 1956, an Elvis wanna-be named Andy Starr attended the WSM Annual Country Music Disc Jockey Festival in Nashville, Tennessee. He was reportedly attacked by girls who thought that he really was Elvis.

1599 The November 8, 1956, issue of the Washington, DC, *Evening Star* newspaper included an article with the headline, "Petition Circulated to Ban Elvis on TV."

1600 Housewives in Syracuse, New York, circulated a petition in November of 1956 asking that Elvis be banned from CBS-TV. The petition was eventually sent to CBS management.

1601 The November 15, 1956, issue of the *New York Journal-American* featured an article entitled, "Elvis Faces Wiggle Ban." The article explained that Louisville, Kentucky, police chief Carl E. Heutis would not permit any "lewd, lascivious contortions that would excite a crowd." Heutis stated, "I just don't happen to be one of his admirers."

1602 The November 15, 1956, issue of the *New York Journal-American* ran an article entitled, "Irate Teenagers Demand Elvis."

1603 The Tupelo *Daily Journal* printed a story in their November 17, 1956, issue entitled "Judge Upholds School's Right to Expel Boy for Wearing Elvis Presley Haircut; Mother May Appeal."

1604 On December 1, 1956, Elvis attended a football game at Crump Stadium in Memphis. He was spotted by the crowd, and it took more than 85 policemen to control the spectators long enough for Elvis to escape.

1605 On November 19, 1956, a doctor at the Iowa Mental Health Institute claimed that Elvis's music actually soothed the mental patients in his hospital.

1606 The song "Old Shep" was released by RCA-Victor in December of 1956 as a promotional record only. It was never released as a regular 45 rpm record.

1607 The December 1956 issue of *Cosmopolitan* magazine featured a story entitled "What Is An Elvis Presley?," written by Eddie Condon.

1608 The December 1956 issue of *TV World* magazine included an article about Elvis entitled "Singer or Sexpot?"

1609 *Modern Screen* magazine's December 1956 issue featured a contest called "Pat [Boone] or Elvis?" Contestants could vote for their favorite singer by mailing in a coupon.

1610   On December 7, 1956, Elvis got a haircut at Jim's Barber Shop, located at 201 S. Main Street in Memphis. Albert Gale had been cutting and styling Elvis's hair since Elvis was a teenager.

1611   James H. Thomas was the owner of Jim's Barber Shop, where Elvis got his hair cut in the mid-1950's. It was located at 201 S. Main Street in Memphis. Thomas and his wife Myrtle lived at 2871 Summer Ave.

1612   Barbers at Jim's Barber Shop included Philip H. Boyd (1338 Jackson Ave), Prentiss C. Lloyd (4385 S. Main), Sylvester Martin (362 Driver, Apt. K), Elem C. Radcliff (535 Pontontoc Ave), and Thomas W. Trigg (1543 Ely).

1613   *Confidential Magazine* printed a hot story about Elvis in their December 1956 issue, claiming that Elvis was in bed with three girls at the same time. Upon seeing the story, Elvis laughed and told his friends that the reporters were only partially right—the actual count was six!

1614   Reverend Carl E. Elgena from Des Moines, Iowa, made this statement on December 3, 1956: "Elvis Presley is morally insane! The spirit of 'Presleyism' has taken down all the bars and standards. We're living in a jellyfish morality!"

1615   *Photoplay* magazine featured the article "Presley Takes Hollywood" in their December 1956 issue.

1616   The December 1956 issue of *Motion Picture* magazine featured an article about Elvis entitled, "The Big Noise From Tupelo."

1617 In December of 1956, Steve Sholes said, "When I met Elvis he was 19. He was wearing a charcoal suit and a pink shirt and on him it looked great. My first impression was that he was an extremely good-looking, warm-hearted, well-mannered, nervous kid. It was his second performance and he was scared. But there was something burning in him. I just looked at him and knew this kid had talent. Actually I should never call Elvis a kid, for as frightened as he was, he went out there and put on a real show. The audience went wild. He really had something!"

1618 Colonel Parker's secretary was Jim O'Brien.

1619 Elvis was photographed for an advertisement for Hungerford Furniture in December of 1956.

1620 The Hungerford Furniture Company had plans to release a line of Elvis Presley furniture in the spring of 1957 that never materialized. The set would have included 40 pieces, from record cabinets to dining room tables, with prices ranging from $39 to $340.

1621 In December of 1956, *The Wall Street Journal* announced that Elvis Presley Enterprises merchandise had grossed $22 million from September to the beginning of December.

1622 When asked during an interview what his biggest thrill was, Elvis replied, "My first gold record."

1623 Approximately 35,000 Elvis singles were sold every day in 1956.

1624 By the end of 1956, 12.5 million Elvis Presley singles and 2.75 million Elvis Presley albums and had been sold.

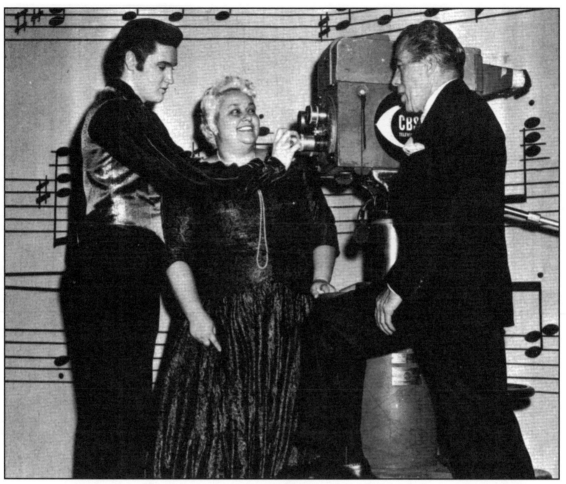

Elvis with Ed Sullivan and Brazilian singer Leny Eversong during Elvis's third appearance on The Ed Sullivan Show, *January 6, 1957.*

1625 Elvis made $1,020,000 from records sales alone in 1956.

1626 On December 21, 1956, Elvis made an appearance on Wink Martindale's "Holiday Hop" show, which aired on KLAC-TV in Memphis.

1627 In 1956, Elvis was quoted as saying, "Fame? It's good. But I won't let it get me. I don't aim to ever let it get me!"

1628 Both the *Roanoke Times* and the *Roanoke World News* newspapers named Elvis "The Hillbilly Frank Sinatra" in 1956/57.

1629 The license plate of Elvis's white Chevy Bel Air convertible was WW-8007 (Tennessee).

1630 In 1956/57, when his popularity had grown to its highest level, Elvis went in search of the 1932 roadster car he had dreamed of owning as a teenager. Unfortunately, he could not find one.

1631 James Scali, chairman of the Custom Tailor Guild, named Elvis Presley and Marlon Brando the "sloppiest celebrities" in 1956/57.

1632 Elvis received 8,000 fan letters a week in 1956/57. He hired several secretaries to answer his mail.

1633 Elvis founded The Elvis Presley Youth Foundation, based in Tupelo, Mississippi, in late 1956/early 1957. He donated $100,000 to the organization each year.

1634 In 1956/57, a California supermarket offered an Elvis 45 rpm record for 29¢ with every $10 purchase. The store made $20,000 before they ran out of records.

1635   In 1956/57, the Colonel made the press pay $500-$1,000 per reporter to interview Elvis and demanded $10,000 for even short radio appearances.

1636   Despite the fact that her son was very rich, Gladys Presley still hand washed her family's laundry with a tub and washboard. She also did all of the ironing by herself and kept herself busy while her son was on the road by mending Vernon's and Elvis's clothes.

1637   Elvis's "Playing For Keeps"/"Too Much" 45 rpm record (47-6800) was released to the public in January of 1957.

1638   For his January 6, 1957, final appearance on *The Ed Sullivan Show*, Elvis took a train from Memphis to New York. He arrived at Penn Station on a Sunday.

1639   Elvis was shown from the waist up on the January 6, 1957, *The Ed Sullivan Show* because his "lewd gyrations" had generated negative response.

1640   For his final *The Ed Sullivan Show* appearance, Elvis sang "Hound Dog," "Love Me Tender," "Heartbreak Hotel," "Don't Be Cruel," "Too Much," "When My Blue Moon Turns to Gold Again," and "Peace in the Valley."

1641   After Elvis's last appearance on *The Ed Sullivan Show*, the Colonel told Ed that if he wanted Elvis for any more appearances the price would be $300,000 per show.

1642   *TV Star Parade* magazine celebrated Elvis's 1957 birthday in conjunction with their own second anniversary. They presented Elvis with a square, chocolate covered cake with the words "Elvis 22 TV Star Parade" written on the top.

1643 On January 7, 1957, Elvis participated in a special promotional photo session for the March of Dimes with the 1956 National Poster Child, Joanne Wilson of Rockaway Beach, New York.

1644 In January of 1957, it was rumored that Elvis was going to have his own TV series in the fall.

1645 Elvis had a recording session on January 12 and 13, 1957, at Radio Recorders in Hollywood, California.

1646 The following nine songs were cut during Elvis's January 1957 recording session in Hollywood: "I Believe," "Tell Me Why," "Got A Lot O' Livin' To Do," "All Shook Up," "Mean Woman Blues," "Peace in the Valley," "I Beg of You," "That's When Your Heartaches Begin," and "Take My Hand, Precious Lord."

1647 On January 15, 1957, approximately 45,000 Elvis fans received the Salk vaccine in honor of their idol. Elvis had received the vaccine on October 28, 1956.

1648 RCA-Victor released the *Strictly Elvis* EP (EPA-994) in January of 1957.

1649 Elvis recorded "It's No Secret," "Blueberry Hill," "Have I Told You Lately That I Love You," and "Is It So Strange" at Radio Recorders on January 19, 1957.

1650 The Thursday, January 24, 1957, issue of the *Miami Herald* newspaper featured a photo of a cat named Elvis Presley.

1651 On January 25, 1957, 16-year-old Ruby Hoff of Atlantic City, New Jersey, had her picture in the paper for being an Elvis Presley fanatic. All four of her bedroom walls were covered with Elvis photos.

1652 The year 1957 saw the largest increase in Elvis Presley Fan Club openings.

1653 Roberta Renee, President of the San Diego, California, Elvis Presley Fan Club, fought with Groucho Marx about Elvis in 1957. Each time Marx said something negative about Elvis on his radio or TV programs, Roberta defended Elvis.

1654 By 1957, there were a reported 250,000 Elvis Presley Fan Club members in the United States alone, with over 85% of the members being teenage girls.

1655 In 1957, there were over 150,000 members in foreign Elvis Presley Fan Clubs.

1656 The February 5, 1957, issue of Tempo magazine (Vol. 8, #3) featured a contest entitled "Tempo Picks Your Rock-n-Roll All-Stars." The results were as follows: 1) Willis Jackson; 2) Bill Haley; 3) Ruth Brown; 4) Chuck Willis; 5) Amos Milburne; 6) The Comets; 7) Elvis Presley; 8) Dinah Washington; 9) Guitar Slim; 10) Fats Domino.

1657 The 1957 "Top Ten Stars of Tomorrow" list included the following people: 1) Anthony Perkins; 2) Sophia Loren; 3) Jayne Mansfield; 4) Don Murray; 5) Carroll Baker; 6) Martha Hyer; 7) Elvis Presley; 8) Anita Ekberg; 9) Paul Newman; 10) John Kerr.

1658 The February 9, 1957, issue of the *Illustrated London News* featured an article entitled "Elvis Presley and the Universal Worship He Engenders," written by A. Bryant.

1659 Mrs. Ruth Brown Moore hired Bosworth Inc. Real Estate to sell her Graceland estate in early 1957. Hugh Bosworth (b. May 23, 1923) of Bosworth Real Estate had sold Elvis his Audubon house in 1956.

1660   All of the rooms in Graceland were designed to be acoustically excellent because the owner's daughter, Grace Moore, was a professional harpist. She went on to play for the Memphis Symphony Orchestra.

1661   A nearby church used the downstairs rooms of Graceland for meetings before Elvis bought the house.

1662   In early February of 1957, Elvis contacted Bosworth Inc., a real estate broker, and spoke with Virginia Grant (b. December 6, 1919) about available properties in the Whitehaven section of Memphis.

1663   At 2:00 p.m. on Tuesday, February 11, 1957, after being shown a ranch-style house similar to his Audubon Drive home, Elvis informed his real estate agent that he was looking for something more grand. The realtor said she would get back to him with a list.

1664   On February 12, 1957, Arthur L. Redner, an assistant professor at Iowa State College in Cedar Falls, stated, "Musical snobs, unsure of their own musicality, narrowly refuse to recognize anything but the highest type of music." He went on to say that those "snobs" were the cause of much criticism of Elvis Presley.

1665   In February of 1957, an Elvis fan from New Orleans, Louisiana, wrote to Memphis City Commissioner Henry Loeb asking that Audubon Drive be renamed Presley Drive. The request was denied.

1666   The February 1957 issue of *Country Song Roundup* (#48) featured a "Presley Word Puzzler Contest — $1,000 Giant." The winner was Aaron Adkins of East Lynn, West Virginia, who won a new RCA-Victor Mark IV High Fidelity consolette.

1667   Elvis usually paid up to $500 for his guitars in the 1950's.

Elvis shaking hands with Marine PFC Hershel Nixon, a sign of peace between the two men. Nixon had reported Elvis for aiming what Nixon thought was a real hand gun at his face on March 25, 1957.

1668   In 1957, Elvis was quoted as saying, "Only food I really enjoy eatin' is my mother's cookin' at home: country ham, black-eyed peas, creamed potatoes, hominy grits, corn pone, hot biscuits, fried corn and okra. Then I can really eat!"

1669   Mack Gurley was a member of Elvis's entourage for a short time in 1957. He first met Elvis in 1954.

1670   Elvis spent $600 in one hour at a ball toss game at the Mid-South Fairgrounds in 1957. He threw the dolls he won into the crowd of screaming fans.

1671   In February of 1957, it was reported that Elvis Presley Enterprises had sold over $26 million worth of merchandise in 1956.

1672   On February 23 and 24, 1957, Elvis recorded the following songs at Radio Recorders in Hollywood: "I Beg of You," "Don't Leave Me Now," "One Night," "True Love," "I Need You So," "Loving You," and "When It Rains It Really Pours."

1673   Elvis's famous gold lamé suit, designed by Nudie Cohen, was made of leather imported from Switzerland. His silver shirt was made of thin kid skin and was lined with silk. Both pieces were custom painted and lined with rhinestones. The suit was made some time in February or March of 1957.

1674   Nudie's Rodeo Tailors of Hollywood was a clothing design company located at 5015 Lankershim Blvd. in North Hollywood, California. Nudie's customers were popular country & western stars. The company later moved to 251 North Beverly Drive in Beverly Hills, where their phone number was (213) 274-3088.

1675   In 1957, Elvis had this to say about his gold lamé suit: "I hate it! It is so heavy, I can hardly stand in it. It's hot and uncomfortable, but it sure damn shines!"

1676   RCA-Victor released the 45 rpm record "All Shook Up"/"That's When Your Heartaches Begin" (47-6870) in March of 1957.

1677   A candy and gum manufacturer made an offer on Elvis's Audubon Drive home in Memphis with the intention of stripping the paneling and sending a piece to anyone who would send in three gum wrappers. Elvis refused to sell to the company.

1678   RCA-Victor released the EP *Peace in the Valley* (EPA-4054) on March 22, 1957.

1679   The Canadian magazine *Liberty* held a WIN A DATE WITH ELVIS contest in their March 1957 issue in which contestants were asked to write a 50 word (or less) essay entitled, "Why Elvis Presley's signing thrills me." The judges were the most popular disc jockeys in Canada, and first prize was a trip to New York, a stay at the luxurious Waldorf-Astoria hotel, a date with Elvis, and a chance to meet other RCA recording artists such as Perry Cuomo.

1680   In March of 1957, Elvis hired real estate agent Hugh Bosworth to sell his 1034 Audubon Drive house. Approximately two weeks after Bosworth was hired, the house sold for $55,000.

1681   Virginia Grant, a realtor who lived at 2315 Douglass Avenue, called Elvis on March 16, 1957, to tell him about a piece of property she wanted to show him in Whitehaven. An appointment to see the house was scheduled for three days later.

1682   Graceland is a two-story white Toshomingo stone building with 23 rooms.

1683   On Monday, March 19, 1957, Elvis met Mrs. Arthur E.(Virginia) Grant in the parking lot of Lowenstein's Department Store, located at the Poplar Plaza Shopping Center on Highland and Poplar Avenue. Grant then took Elvis and his parents to see Graceland for the first time.

1684   When Elvis first saw the interior of Graceland, he said, "...it was filled with cobwebs and the plaster was cracked!" Major work had to be done before the mansion would be livable.

1685   When Elvis discovered that the Memphis YMCA had bid $35,000 for the Graceland estate, he put in his own bid: $100,000!

1686   After Elvis selected and bought 13.75 acres of the Graceland estate, he offered the city of Memphis the chance to buy the remaining acres.

1687   The agreement Elvis signed to buy Graceland entitled him to 13.75 acres and the city of Memphis to the other 486.25 acres.

1688   On March 25, 1957, Elvis and Marine private Hershel Nixon had a confrontation over Elvis having bumped into Nixon's wife a few months earlier. Elvis pulled out a studio prop gun and the police were called. Fortunately, things calmed down and the end result was captured in a photo of Elvis and Nixon shaking hands.

1689   At 4:30 p.m. on March 26, 1957, the paperwork was signed and Elvis's deal to purchase Graceland was closed.

1690   To cover the balance of the $100,000 price tag not covered by the sale of his Audubon Drive home, Elvis put a $10,000 deposit on Graceland and took a $37,000 mortgage from Equitable Life with a 4% interest rate.

1691 The sale of Graceland was closed in the law offices of Evans, Petree & Cobb, located in the 647 Commerce Title Building in Memphis. Their phone number was 37-6322.

1692 When Elvis purchased Graceland in 1957, Whitehaven had 15,000 residents.

1693 On March 28, 1957, just two days after buying Graceland, Elvis hired George Golden as his interior designer.

1694 George Golden was a 43-year-old man who had once been a Lipton Tea salesman. After decorating Graceland, he did some work for Sam Phillips.

1695 George Golden bought most of the decorating materials for Graceland at Goldsmith's Department Store, located at 4545 Poplar Avenue in Memphis.

1696 George Golden decorated Graceland in royal blue, white, and gold.

1697 Elvis had green shutters put on all the windows at Graceland.

1698 Elvis and Gladys put up a large white mailbox outside the Graceland gates. On the box was written "Graceland, 3764 US Highway 51 So., Memphis 16, Tenn."

1699 Elvis commissioned George Golden to do two specific things to Graceland: install a professional soda fountain (with three flavors of ice cream) and design the best bedroom ever.

1700 The soda fountain at Graceland cost Elvis $3,000!

1701 Elvis bought furniture for Graceland from numerous stores, though much of it came from Donald's, a store in Memphis.

1702 Donald's Furniture Co., Inc., was located at 405 N. Cleveland in Memphis. The president was Irvin H. Pelts and its vice president was Kenneth D. Menkel. Their telephone number in the 1950's was 2-1286.

1703 Graceland's front door is made of oak and stands 10 feet tall.

1704 Elvis had a stained glass window panel with the letter "P" surrounded by red roses installed above the front door at Graceland.

1705 Elvis once said that the Presleys' entire Tupelo house could have fit into Graceland's living room.

1706 Graceland had a four car garage when Elvis purchased the estate.

1707 Elvis bought a full-sized pool table for his recreation room at Graceland. His favorite billiard games were "8-Ball" and "Rotation."

1708 The gas fireplace in the living room at Graceland was made of white Italian marble.

1709 When Elvis purchased Graceland, his electrician was George Coleman.

1710 There were pecan trees growing on the grounds of Graceland when Elvis purchased the property.

1711 Elvis had the garage at Graceland converted into a large den and had a carport built to accommodate his fleet of vehicles.

Elvis with disc jockey Dewey Phillips at WHBQ Radio in Memphis, 1957.
Phillips is showing Elvis how he used glue to mend a broken copy of "All Shook Up."

1712   The four white Corinthian columns in front of Graceland are of a design called "The Temple of the Winds."

1713   Elvis's bedroom at Graceland included a black leather bed and dresser, a white rug, a white satin bedspread, white corduroy drapes, a white ceiling, three dark blue walls, and one mirrored wall.

1714   Elvis had a gold phone in his Graceland bedroom.

1715   In the 1950's, Elvis had a carved Indian chief statue in his bedroom at Graceland.

1716   Elvis's private bathroom in Graceland was decorated with pink and orchid colors. The shower doors boasted his initials on the glass panels.

1717   Elvis's telephone number at Graceland was 397-4427.

1718   Gladys Presley grew tomatoes in the back yard at Graceland.

1719   A peach tree originally grew on the grounds at Graceland, but when the acreage was surveyed and divided between Elvis and the city of Memphis, the tree was discovered to be on someone else's property.

1720   Gladys Presley had wallpaper printed with poodles installed in the bedroom she and Vernon shared at Graceland.

1721   Minnie Mae Presley's bedroom at Graceland was lilac-colored. In it she displayed photos of Elvis, Gladys, and Anita Wood, one of Elvis's long-time girlfriends.

1722   After Elvis bought Graceland, surrounding properties sold for $1,500 per 5 acres.

1723   Alice Smith was one of Elvis's Graceland neighbors.

1724   Elvis owned a mini zoo at Graceland. He had twenty chickens, eight ducks, six guinea pigs, five Scottish terriers, two peacocks, two hogs, two burros, two pet monkeys, two miniature French poodles, Gladys's Pomeranian, and a turkey.

1725   Elvis's pet turkey, Bow-Tie, got his name from three dark feathers growing under his neck that were shaped like a bow tie.

1726   Elvis received two burros from Colonel Parker, who sent them to Elvis from Texas.

1727   One of Elvis's favorite pets was a fuzzy, black spider monkey named Jayhew.

1728   Elvis once had a white Great Pyrenees named Muffin. Unfortunately the dog suffered permanent injuries at an obedience school and had to be put to sleep.

1729   Elvis had a bowl of goldfish in his office at Graceland; he loved to watch them swim around aimlessly.

1730   Elvis bought two horses in 1957, one of which was named Diamond. Both turned out to be mean and were not fond of their new owner.

1731   On March 28, 1957, Elvis held a press conference at the Saddle and Sirloin Club of the Stockyard Inn, located near the International Amphitheater in Chicago, Illinois.

1732   As part of a local contest, a lucky girl won a ticket to Elvis's press conference at the Saddle and Sirloin Club in March of 1957.

1733 On April 3, 1957, Elvis received a silver and gold Indian medallion on a chain from a fan from Ottawa, Canada.

1734 The April 3, 1957 issue of the *Hamilton Spectator* newspaper carried the headline "Presley Brings Delirium Tremors to 25,000!"

1735 In April of 1957, Elvis stated that he owned eight cars: four Cadillacs, one Lincoln Continental, and three sports cars.

1736 On April 6, 1957, Elvis held a press conference at the Philadelphia Sports Arena in Philadelphia, Pennsylvania.

1737 Elvis wore the silver and gold Indian medallion sent to him by a Canadian fan to his Philadelphia press conference held on April 6, 1957.

1738 John Dillars, Sr. and Abe Saucer designed Elvis's famous music gates at Graceland.

1739 The music gates were installed at Graceland on April 6, 1957.

1740 The notes on the Graceland gates are the first notes from "Love Me Tender."

1741 The company that installed the music gates at Graceland was Doors Inc., located at 911 Rayner in Memphis. The company's phone number was 272-3046.

1742 It was rumored that the music gates at Graceland cost Elvis $2,400.

1743 Graceland's first gate guard was Travis Smith, Elvis's uncle.

Elvis checking out new records at Popular Tunes Record Shop in Memphis.

1744   Vester Presley worked as a gate guard at Graceland from 1957 to 1982. Gladys's brothers, Travis and John, also worked as gate guards. The first tours of Graceland began in 1957, with Vester taking groups of fans up to the house and walking them around the grounds.

1745   On April 9, 1957, Elvis's cousin, Gene Smith, married Louise Fondren.

1746   The April 27, 1957, issue of England's *Melody Maker* magazine included an article by H. Whiston entitled "Elvis Forgot the Holes in His Socks."

1747   Elvis had a special king-sized bed made for his room at Graceland, complete with drawers and a 9-foot canopy. The bed was made by cabinet makers J.E., Andre, and Ray McCollough on April 29, 1957.

1748   In the 1950's, Elvis enjoyed eating corn dogs dipped in mustard.

1749   In May of 1957, Elvis hired C.W. Nichols to paint Graceland.

1750   C.W. Nichols gave Elvis a poodle, which Elvis named Hugo.

1751   The Painters Union Local 49 picketed outside Graceland because Elvis hired a non-union contractor to paint Graceland in 1957.

1752   The 6-foot wall around Graceland was made of Alabama fieldstone and cost Elvis $30,000!

1753   Elvis's Graceland wall was built by union bricklayers.

1754   Elvis originally had four rows of barbed wire installed along the top of the wall at Graceland. It was removed when several fans hurt themselves.

1755 Before Elvis had the pool at Graceland filled with water, he used it as a corral for the donkeys he had received from fans.

1756 Sara Erwin, a school teacher, was a neighbor of Elvis's at Graceland.

1757 One of Elvis's neighbors at Graceland was Mrs. E.P. Inderbitzen.

1758 Gladys and Vernon Presley took daily morning walks around Graceland.

1759 Wayne Williams was once Elvis's paper boy at Graceland. He graduated from Whitehaven High School in 1958.

1760 In the 1950's, James Burns was the Presleys' postman at Graceland. The 63-year-old man lived at 5162 Airways Blvd.

1761 Lamar Fike and Cliff Gleaves, both Elvis's friends and members of his entourage, lived at Graceland for a time in 1957.

1762 The May 1957 issue of *Hit Parader* magazine featured a list of the top songs in the country. Sonny James's "Young Love" was #1 in the South; Mickey & Sylvia's "Love is Strange" was #1 in the Mid-West; Elvis Presley's "Too Much" was #1 in the West; and Johnnie Ray's "You Don't Owe Me a Thing" was #1 in the East.

1763 On May 15, 1957, Elvis was rushed to Cedars of Lebanon Hospital; he had inhaled one of his tooth caps. A special procedure was used to remove the porcelain cap from his lung.

1764 The two nurses who took care of Elvis when he was hospitalized in May of 1957 were Beverly Altomore and Elissa Martyn.

1765 *Movieland* magazine featured an "Elvis Presley Photo Contest" in their May 1957 issue (Vol. 15, #5). Contestants had to send in their own photo of Elvis, along with a coupon from the magazine which included date, place, type of camera used, etc. First prize was $25, second prize was $20, third prize was $15, and the following ten prizes were $10 each. The contest was directed by editor Dorothea Lee McEvoy.

1766 The results of *Movieland* magazine's first Elvis photo contest were as follows: first place — Margaret Octavia Wynne of South Boston, Virginia; second place — Janet Sue Guinane of Houston, Texas; third place — Arthur Mensor of Los Altos, California; runner up — Sylvia Helena Oriold of Toronto, Canada.

1767 *Movie Teen Illustrated* magazine ran a contest called "Win a Free Elvis Presley Oil Painting" in the summer of 1957. Contestants had to write a short letter describing a party idea; the winner won the oil painting and the party of their choice.

1768 In 1957, Elvis sent a telegram to Ted Crutchfield, a disc jockey with WCMS Radio, thanking him for having an Elvis Presley Day on his station.

1769 There were six major record labels in 1957: RCA-Victor, Capitol, Decca, MGM, Columbia, and Mercury.

1770 Colonel Parker did not register Elvis with the musical firms ASCAP or BMI in the 1950's or 1960's.

1771 Elvis frequently chewed gum during the 1950's. He had a particular fondness for Doublemint gum.

1772 Elvis's cousin, Wayne Presley, spent a good deal of time at Graceland. He also attended some of Elvis's movie theater and amusement parties.

1773　A teenager had to be rushed to the hospital in 1957 after dislocating his pelvis with too much Elvis-style dancing.

1774　Elvis wore 1956 Elvis Presley Enterprises sneakers while playing football with his friends in 1957. He wore the white sneakers with black print.

1775　From 1957 through the 1970's, Elvis bought several of his Cadillacs from Madison Cadillac, located on Union Avenue in Memphis.

1776　In 1957, Elvis had nightmares about being killed by several men. He was so scared by these dreams that he started having his entourage escort him everywhere.

1777　Elizabeth McCormick was Elvis's secretary in the 1950's and 1960's.

1778　Sisters Oralee (age 15) and Sharyn (age 14) Davoli covered their bedroom walls with 1,087 photos of Elvis in 1957.

1779　In 1957, the Chrysler Corporation wanted Elvis to drive one of their cars. They offered free cars to his band members, but Elvis and the Colonel still declined the offer.

1780　In the 1950's, RCA Appliances wanted Elvis to endorse their products. They offered free state-of-the-art appliances for payment, but the Colonel told them to stop bothering Elvis and his band.

1781　A promotional 16-inch transcription record (GM-BM-0653) of Elvis promoting the March of Dimes was released by RCA-Victor. Called 1957 *March of Dimes—Galaxy of Stars*, the record featured statements from stars, an interview with Elvis, and Elvis's "Love Me Tender."

1782 By 1957, Elvis had spent so much time at Chenault's Restaurant that the manager set up a private dining room for him. Chenault's was located at 1402 South Bellevue Blvd. in Memphis.

1783 In 1957, Elvis said that Calypso music and marriage were the two things farthest from his mind.

1784 In 1957, Elvis stated that his first album (*Elvis Presley*, LPM-1254) had sold more albums than any other in RCA's history!

1785 In 1957, Elvis said that his favorite songs were "I Was the One" and "Tryin' To Get To You."

1786 Dr. Edward Kantor (b. March 20, 1911) of Beverly Hills, California, served as Elvis's eye, ear, and nose specialist from 1957 on.

1787 In 1957, Elvis's records were sold on the Russian black market for $12.50 (US dollars).

1788 In 1957, Elvis's record sales, souvenir sales, and concert admissions totaled $120 million.

1789 Elvis stated that he was Italian and Irish in 1957.

1790 In 1957, Elvis bought 1,400 tickets to a football game at Crump Stadium and donated them to L.C. Humes High School. Although all of the students from his alma mater were invited to the game, Elvis himself did not go.

1791 One day in 1957, Elvis got so angry that he threw an expensive guitar down a hotel hallway. The guitar was completely ruined when it splintered after hitting a wall.

*At Graceland, Gladys sits in her famous pink Cadillac as Elvis and Yvonne Lime
share in the excitement.*

1792   Two men hired by Elvis in 1957 were with his entourage for such a short period of time that their names are barely known. Louis Harris worked for Elvis for about eight months; Tommy Young worked for Elvis for about six months.

1793   There are no photos of Gladys Presley alone with the Colonel. She did not like Parker and refused to pose with him.

1794   In 1957, Gladys said that she was the most miserable person in the world. She said she couldn't go shopping or out to the movies because of Elvis's fame, and she hardly got to see her son because he was always on tour.

1795   *The Canadian Home Journal* featured the headline "What is Presley Doing To Our Children?" in its June 1957 issue.

1796   The first Elvis Presley game was manufactured by Teen-Age Games Inc. in West Springfield, Massachusetts, in 1957. There were five levels in The Elvis Presley Game: "Getting to Know Him," "Learning to Like Him," "Can't Do Without Him," "Let's Go Steady," and "Get the Preacher."

1797   In the late 1950's, one of Elvis's oldest fans was 103 years old!

1798   In the late 1950's, Elvis liked the scent of White Shoulders perfume on women.

1799   It was said that Elvis never wore the same outfit twice. His family and friends stated that he had more clothes in his closet than were in Lansky's store.

1800   In 1957, there were two female Elvis Presley impersonators in the United States: Sparkle Moore and Alis Lesley.

1801 Elvis developed some kind of skin infection near his shoulder in 1957. A doctor prescribed a special ointment, and, about two weeks later, the infection cleared up.

1802 Tennessee Williams's 1957 book, *Orpheus Descending*, was said to be about Elvis Presley. The book was about a god named Orpheus whose music captured the public; Orpheus was ultimately destroyed by idolatry and corruption.

1803 Elvis made an impromptu, secret visit to a party being held for cerebral palsy patients in 1957.

1804 Columnist Vernon Scott produced a list of the traits and habits of "super stars" in 1957. He called Elvis the "Most Secretive."

1805 Elvis was introduced to tanning pills in 1957.

1806 At Temple University in Pennsylvania, an English professor held a lengthy debate comparing Elvis Presley and William Shakespeare.

1807 Glenna Anderson, a 14-year-old member of the Lakeside 4-H Club, had a steer named "Elvis." He won the "Best Steer" ribbon at the East San Diego County Fair, where his competitors were "Royal" and "Fats Domino."

1808 Mexican education minister Jose Angel Ceniceros banned Elvis, his music, and his movies from Mexico in 1957 after he heard the rumor that "Elvis would rather kiss three black women than one Mexican one." The rumor was not true.

1809 A Mexican newspaper carried this headline in 1957: "Death to Elvis Presley!"

1810   In 1957, sugar heiress Judy Spreckles, one of Elvis's close friends, became ill with blood poisoning. She also broke off her engagement to a gentleman from the South.

1811   When Russia's Nikita Khrushchev started being anti-everyone in 1957, Milton Berle was quoted as saying, "The way I figure it, Khrushchev is trying to prove that he's Russia's answer to Elvis Presley!"

1812   In 1957, a 200-pound hog named "Elvis" was chosen as Champion Barrow in the Junior Feeding Contest at the International Livestock Exposition in Chicago, Illinois.

1813   It was reported that Elvis was learning how to body surf from female skin-diving champion Zale Perry in 1957.

1814   Elvis's nickname in China in 1957 was "Mow Wang," which translates to "King Cat."

1815   The license plate number on Elvis's 1957 black Cadillac was 2D-33501 (Tennessee).

1816   In 1957, the Colonel turned down several $40,000 offers for Elvis to appear on various television shows. When asked why he rejected the offers, Parker was quoted as saying, "If people can see him for nothing on TV, how can I get $250,000 a picture for him?"

1817   In the summer of 1957, Colonel Parker demanded $10,000 from a New York Sunday magazine after they asked if they could feature Elvis on their front cover. They declined to pay.

1818   During the summer of 1957, Elvis went to the Monsignor Restaurant in Hollywood, California. No one recognized him when he walked in, but when Maurice Chevalier came in, everyone applauded.

1819 Elvis went to the Ellis Auditorium in July of 1957, where he spotted a beautiful white Knabe piano. He struck a deal with the management, bought the piano, and purchased a replacement for the Auditorium.

1820 In July of 1957, Elvis was featured on the cover of three magazines: *Photoplay*, *Star Parade*, and *TV Life*.

1821 On July 27, 1957, England's *Melody Maker* magazine featured an article by C. O'Curran entitled "At Last the Truth About Elvis."

1822 In August of 1957 Elvis and Dewey Phillips had a fight. Elvis claimed that Dewey was low-class and Dewey claimed that Elvis was a Hollywood snob.

1823 In August of 1957, Tennessee governor Buford Ellington bestowed the honorary title of "Colonel" on Elvis.

1824 Gladys Presley had a Siamese cat named Wendell Corey.

1825 Elvis's two miniature French poodles were named Duke and Pierre.

1826 On August 31, 1957, Elvis held a press conference in Vancouver, British Columbia. It was held in the Lion's football dressing room, located in the lower side of the Empire Stadium. Red Robinson served as the interviewer and the emcee.

1827 *Movie Teen Illustrated* magazine ran a "Win a Trip to Memphis" contest in the fall of 1957. Contestants were required to write a letter describing themselves and their qualifications; entries were sent to the "Am I the Girl for Elvis Department."

1828 Elvis was asked to sing at the Academy Awards in 1957, but when the Colonel demanded a $40,000 fee, the Academy took back their offer.

1829 Elvis sported a guitar-shaped chrome watch in the late 1950's.

1830 The 1950's book The Elvis Presley Story, written by James Gregory, featured an introduction by Dick Clark.

1831 Marion Keisker and Sam Phillips had a big fight in September of 1957. She quit her job as his secretary and joined the U.S. Air Force.

1832 When Sam Phillips sold Sun Studios, it was reported that he had earned approximately two million dollars from the songs and artists he worked with in the 1950's.

1833 Sam Phillips' younger brother, Jerry, was once a midget mud wrestler. He performed in Arkansas under the name Delane Phillips.

1834 RCA-Victor released the *Just For You* EP (EPA-4041) in September of 1957.

1835 Some time in 1957, Elvis was offered an outrageous amount of money to shave off his sideburns with an electric razor on television. Elvis said no!

1836 In 1957, Elvis was ranked #4 at the United States box office. Frank Sinatra was right behind Elvis at #5, and Rock Hudson topped the list at #1.

Elvis sits in his exotic 3-wheeled Messerschmidt car, 1957.

1837 In the fall of 1957, Elvis received a $900,000 royalty from the sale of 1956 Elvis Presley Enterprises merchandise—and that amount was earned in only fifteen months!

1838 On October 23, 1957, George Klein interviewed Elvis for his Memphis-based WHBQ Radio program.

1839 In October of 1957, while at a special event to promote a high school championship football game, Elvis donated $15,000 to the Foundation for the Blind. All proceeds from the game, which was to be held on Thanksgiving Day, also went to the foundation.

1840 The November 2, 1957, issue of England's *Melody Maker* magazine featured an article by H. Lucraft entitled "Elvis Says 'I've Never Written A Song.'"

1841 On November 9, 1957, Elvis was quoted as saying, "I don't like airplanes! I'm scared stiff of them!"

1842 Elvis was interviewed by Tom Moffat of KPOI Radio in Honolulu, Hawaii, on November 10, 1957.

1843 On November 23, 1957, in the Shalimar Room of the Commodore Perry Hotel in Toledo, Ohio, 19-year-old Louis John Balint punched Elvis in the face.

1844 Ohio police officers William Kina and Walter Zalazynski answered the call when Elvis was punched by Louis Balint.

1845 The fight between Elvis and Louis Balint in 1957 was actually staged! Colonel Parker paid Balint $200 to punch Elvis, which Parker thought would "add controversy to Elvis's career."

1846   Louis John Balint, whom Colonel Parker approached to stage the 1957 fight with Elvis in Toledo, had worked as a steelworker since 1956.

1847   In 1957 and 1958, when Elvis first began renting the Rainbow Skate Rink, located at 2881 Lamar Avenue in Memphis, he was charged 50¢ for admission and 25¢ for rental per person.

1848   The owners of the Rainbow Skate Rink in Memphis where Elvis held his skating parties were Joseph P. and Doris E. Pieraccini, who lived at 761 N. Auburndale in Memphis.

1849   Elvis eventually worked out a flat fee rental of $35 per night for his skating parties with the owners of the Rainbow Skate Rink. This price included skates, food, and drinks for everyone.

1850   Elvis's skating parties began around midnight and lasted until the early hours of the morning.

1851   Elvis always wore blue jeans to his skating parties; this was the only time he wore jeans.

1852   One of Elvis's favorite skating games was "Pop the Whip," which involved forming a line and turning sharply so that the last person in line would be whipped off.

1853   Elvis enjoyed the skating game "War," which entailed two sides crashing into each other in an attempt to knock each other down. This game was played until only one person was left standing.

1854   Elvis and his friends often ate in the Terrace Room of the Rainbow Skate Rink in Memphis.

1855 Elvis and his friends often visited the Handy Theater, an R&B club located at Park Avenue and Airways Blvd. in Memphis. The theater was named after William Christopher "W.T." Handy, one of the pioneers of the blues.

1856 Students at the University of Southern California named Elvis the "most popular movie personality of the year" in 1957.

1857 In 1957, *Variety* magazine's "Top Talent of the Month" listed Elvis at #1 with his songs "All Shook Up," "Peace in the Valley," and "That's When Your Heartaches Begin."

1858 Elvis enjoyed having fireworks at Graceland during holidays and on the Fourth of July.

1859 Elvis's favorite fireworks were 16-shot Roman candles. For protection against the Roman candles, he and his gang used garbage can lids as shields.

1860 The Colonel boasted of writing a book called *The Benevolent Con Man — How Much Does It Cost If It's Free*, but he never got around to it.

1861 The license plate number on Elvis's 1957 white Cadillac Seville convertible was WW-8007 (Tennessee).

1862 On December 14, 1957, Elvis acquired the land on Old Saltillo Road in Tupelo where he was born. The city of Memphis persuaded Orville Bean to sell the land to Elvis for $500. The land was used to restore Elvis's birthplace and to build the Elvis Presley Youth and Recreation Center.

1863 The songwriters and publishers of "Heartbreak Hotel," "Hound Dog," and "Don't Be Cruel" were engaged in fights over the song rights.

Songwriters included Mae Axton and Tommy Durden for "Heartbreak Hotel," Jerry Leiber and Mike Stoller for "Hound Dog," and Otis Blackwell for "Don't Be Cruel."

1864 Hill & Range Music purchased and established several music publishing companies for Elvis, including American Music, now known as the American Division of Elvis Presley Music, Inc.

1865 In late 1957, Elvis was asked to appear on *The Big Record TV* show. When the Colonel demanded a fee of $75,000, the show rescinded the offer.

1866 Barbara Barnes Sims worked for Sun Studios from 1957 to 1960. She set up a fan club for Elvis and answered his fan mail.

1867 Over $55 million worth of Elvis Presley Enterprises merchandise was in the homes of Elvis fans by the end of 1957.

1868 In January of 1958, RCA raised the price of their 45rpm records from 89¢ to 98¢.

1869 For Elvis's 23rd birthday (January 8, 1958), his friends threw him a party at a hotel in downtown Memphis. Afterwards, everyone went roller-skating at the Rainbow Skate Rink.

1870 The January 1958 issue of *Harper's* magazine featured an article called "Man in Blue Suede Shoes" by J. Baxter.

1871 On January 9, 1958, Elvis held a photo session at Graceland with 8-year-old Mary Kosloski, the 1955 National Polio Poster Child for the March of Dimes. Along with thanking Elvis for his sizable donations, Mary also wished him a happy 23rd birthday.

1872 Elvis's "I Beg Of You"/"Don't" 45 rpm record was released to the public in January of 1958.

1873 On January 23, 1958, Elvis tried to record "My Wish Came True" and "Doncha' Think It's Time" at Radio Recorders in Hollywood. After three hours, however, nothing was coming out right and everyone went home.

1874 Elvis attempted to record "Doncha' Think It's Time" forty times on January 23, 1958, before RCA called it quits.

1875 After an unsuccessful session a week earlier, Elvis was called back to the recording studio on February 1, 1958, to cut "My Wish Came True," "Doncha' Think It's Time," "Your Cheatin' Heart," and "Wear My Ring Around Your Neck."

1876 It took 22 takes to get "Wear My Ring Around Your Neck" right.

1877 In March of 1958, Elvis bought every member of his entourage a pair of cowboy boots with thick heels, known then as "elevator heels."

1878 Gladys Presley began to suffer from menopause in March of 1958.

1879 *The Phil Silvers Show* rebroadcast the "Rock and Roll Rookie" episode, a parody of Elvis, on March 28, 1958.

1880 *The Hy Gardner Calling* show featuring Elvis was shown for the second time on New York TV station WABD (Channel 5) on March 30, 1958.

1881 In 1958, members of Elvis Presley Fan Clubs boycotted Tommy Sands' movie *Sing Boy Sing*. It was rumored that Elvis was up for the role, an Elvis-like character whom the fans hated seeing Sands play.

Billy Smith, Elvis's cousin. From a promotional postcard.

1882 Elvis won the *TV Star Parade* "Favorite Singer Contest" in 1958.

1883 The album *Elvis's Golden Records* (LPM-1707) was released in April of 1958. It featured fourteen of Elvis's million-selling hits.

1884 "Wear My Ring Around Your Neck"/"Doncha' Think It's Time" was released as a 45 rpm single (47-7240) in April of 1958.

1885 On April 5, 1958, *DISC* column writer Jack Good wrote, "Elvis Presley is a giant because he has taken the sex in rock-n-roll as far as it can go. They don't come more sexy than Elvis!"

1886 *Teen Magazine* ran a "Mister Number One" poll in their April 1958 issue. Elvis finished first, beating Ricky Nelson (#2), Johnny Mathis (#3), Pat Boone (#4) and Perry Como (#5).

1887 In 1958, Elvis said that he could not read music or play the guitar. He said he used a guitar for balance and to busy his nervous hands.

1888 In 1958, the Russian black market sold Elvis records for $50 each!

1889 In the 1950's, Elvis's records were sold on the black market in East Germany, Poland, and other Communist countries.

1890 Delbert "Sonny" West met Elvis at the Rainbow Skate Rink in 1958. He soon joined his cousin, Red, in protecting Elvis from his fans.

1891 Sonny West quit his job at the Ace Appliance Company when he went to work for Elvis full time in 1958.

1892 Sterling Gary Pepper, Jr. (b. May 14, 1931), a very special friend of Elvis's, and his parents, Sterling (b. December 12, 1901) and Nell

(Lucas) Pepper (b. December 28, 1900), lived at 793 Eva in Memphis. In 1950, Sterling Pepper was a route superintendent.

1893 Hull-Dobbs Ford Co., where Elvis purchased a few cars, was located at 3rd Street at Gayoso Avenue in Memphis. The company's telephone number was 8-8871. The president of Hull-Dobbs Ford Co. was Horace H. Hull. Vice presidents included James K. Dobbs, Oscar T. Oakley, James K. Dobbs, Jr., and Charles H. Hull. The secretary was Frank Goodwin.

1894 Elvis's cousin, Carroll Jay "Junior" Smith, died of a heart attack in 1958. Although he lived at 736 Craft Road at the time, Junior died at his Uncle Travis's house, located at 4935 Fairley Road in Whitehaven.

1895 Elvis took care of all funeral expenses for his cousin, Junior Smith, when he died in 1958.

1896 In 1958, Elvis bought an apricot-colored French toy poodle from a kennel in Wembley Park, Middlesex, England. The dog's named was "Teddy Bear of Zizipompom" and he cost $281.

1897 In 1958, Elvis made the following statement about imitators: "I enjoy it more than anybody else does. You've got to have a sense of humor in this business. When you start taking yourself seriously, you're in trouble. Sammy Davis, Jr. does one of the best impersonations of me I've ever seen, but there are several other artists almost as funny. I enjoy them all!"

1898 In 1958, Elvis won popularity polls as the #1 singer in Cairo, Egypt, and Iraq.

1899 *Teen* magazine held their annual "Teen Survey Bureau Poll" in June of 1958. Elvis was selected as #2 on the "Top Pop Poll Champions List" for "Mister Number One." The #1 position went to Ricky Nelson.

1900   Gladys and Vernon Presley celebrated their 25th wedding anniversary on June 17, 1958.

1901   In 1958, a London newspaper stated that Elvis fans received lower marks in school than Pat Boone fans, Perry Como fans, and Frank Sinatra fans!

1902   In 1958, the address of the Elvis Presley Youth and Recreation Center was PO Box 331, Tupelo, Mississippi.

1903   By June of 1958, 78 rpm records were abandoned entirely; interest was focused on LPs and 45 rpm records.

1904   Elvis's final recording session in the 1950's occurred on June 10 and 11, 1958, at the RCA studio in Nashville, Tennessee.

1905   Elvis recorded "I Need Your Love Tonight," "A Big Hunk O' Love," "Ain't That Loving You Baby," "A Fool Such as I," and "I Got Stung" during the summer of 1958 session at RCA in Nashville.

1906   The following musicians were used for Elvis's final 1950's recording session: guitar—Walter Hank Garland, Chet Atkins, and Elvis Presley; bass—Bob L. Moore; drums—DJ Fontana; bongos—Murray "Buddy" Harman; piano—Floyd Cramer; vocals—The Jordanaires.

1907   Neither Scotty Moore nor Bill Black were used for Elvis's June 1958 recording session.

1908   It was reported that Elvis was sued for $5000 by a female resident of Washington, DC, in July of 1958. She claimed Elvis had damaged her car by crashing into her.

Uncle Travis Smith, one of the first gate guards at Graceland, 1957. He was Gladys's brother.

1909   In 1958, gumball dispensers gave out a little photo card of Elvis, made by Elvis Presley Enterprises, after a penny was deposited.

1910   Gladys Presley had her first hepatitis attack on August 9, 1958.

1911   The doctors diagnosed Gladys Presley with acute hepatitis on the day of her first attack.

1912   Gladys Presley's private doctor in Memphis was Dr. Charles Clarke. Dr. Clarke's birth date was February 13, 1912.

1913   Gladys Presley was in and out of consciousness while in the hospital on Monday, August 11, 1958.

1914   On the morning of August 13, 1958, Gladys Presley suffered a mild heart attack. Doctors at Methodist Hospital examined her and announced that she was fine, even though they drained about a gallon and a half of excess fluid from her body that day.

1915   When Elvis arrived at Methodist Hospital on August 13, 1958, Gladys reached for him and said, "My son, my son!" with great difficulty.

1916   At the hospital the day before Gladys Presley died, the doctors said she was doing well and, if her condition continued to improve, she could be released in a few days.

1917   The Methodist Hospital where Gladys died was located at 1265 Union Avenue. The hospital's phone number was 36-3361. James M. Crews was hospital superintendent.

1918   Gladys Presley's last words to Elvis were, "Be careful, son."

1919 Moments before Gladys Presley died, she struggled for breath. When Vernon heard her gasping, he called for a nurse. Although an oxygen tent was sent for immediately, it was too late.

1920 Gladys Love Smith Presley suffered a second heart attack and died at 3:15 a.m. on August 14, 1958, in room 688 of Methodist Hospital in Memphis.

1921 Betty McMahan was a nurse working at the hospital when Gladys Presley died. She was also one of Elvis's first girlfriends.

1922 Red West's father, Newton Thomas West, died at 10:00 a.m. on August 14, 1958, the same day as Gladys Presley.

1923 Neither Elvis nor Vernon would allow an autopsy to be performed on Gladys.

1924 Preparations for Gladys Presley's funeral were arranged by the National Funeral Home, located at 1177 Union Avenue in Memphis.

1925 The National Funeral Home's phone number was 2-2112 and Omer E. Bisplinghoff was the manager. The director of the funeral home was Douglas P. Cross (1359 Linden Ave, Apt. 44); the embalmers were Wayne Cline (757 Roland), L. Aubrey Coleman (986 Ave, Apt. 3), and Roy G. Fisher (507 E. McLemore Ave.).

1926 Gladys Presley was laid out in a baby blue dress and soft slippers before being placed in her coffin.

1927 Elvis spared no expense for his mother's funeral. He ordered a custom-made, copper-colored casket for her. The entire funeral cost $19,000.

1928 Elvis had the National Funeral Home place a clear glass covering over his mother's coffin so that people could see but not touch her.

1929 On August 15, 1958, Gladys lay in state at Graceland. After the wake, Elvis opened the coffin and threw himself on Gladys's body, crying, "Wake up, Mama! Wake up!" Vernon had to pull his son away and doctors gave Elvis a strong sedative.

1930 Upon her death, over 1,000 people came to the National Funeral Home to pay their respects to Elvis's mother. Due to the massive size of the crowd, more than 65 policemen were ordered to guard the building.

1931 On Friday, August 16, 1958, Gladys was taken to the Forest Hill Cemetery for burial. A 100 car procession followed behind. The cemetery is located about two and a half miles from Graceland.

1932 Forest Hill Cemetery was located at 1804 Mississippi Blvd., and the cemetery telephone number was 9-6601. It had two entrances: one at Mississippi Blvd. and the other at Bellevue Blvd.

1933 The Forest Hill Cemetery slogan was "Naturally beautiful— Beautifully kept."

1934 The president of the Forest Hill Cemetery was George D. Mitchell, vice president was A. Walton Ketchum, and secretary was Mrs. Irene R. Daniel.

1935 Reverend James E. Hamill gave the eulogy and performed the funeral service for Gladys Presley.

1936 At Gladys's funeral, the Blackwood Brothers Gospel Quartet sang Gladys's favorite song, "Precious Memories," and some of her other favorite hymns, "Rock of Ages," "In the Garden," and "I Am Redeemed."

1937 Over 3,000 mourners attended Gladys Presley's funeral on August 16, 1958. All passed her casket; approximately 400 squeezed into the chapel for services.

1938 As his mother's coffin was lowered into the ground, it took several people to hold Elvis back from jumping in after her.

1939 Elvis had to be assisted in walking and standing throughout his mother's funeral.

1940 Gladys Presley had an honor guard at her funeral.

1941 Vernon objected to Elvis putting a Star of David on Gladys's grave, but Elvis was adamant about celebrating his mother's Jewish heritage.

1942 Elvis had the Star of David placed on the left side and the Cross on the right side of her name on Gladys's gravestone in honor of both her Jewish ancestry and her Protestant religion.

1943 Written on Gladys's original gravestone was the following:
✡ Gladys Smith Presley ✝
April 25, 1912 — August 14, 1958
Beloved Wife of Vernon Presley
and Mother of Elvis Presley
"She was the sunshine of our home"

1944 Gladys Presley's headstone, rectangular in shape and made of dark marble, was made by White Monument, located at Bellevue and South Parkway in Memphis.

1945 Neither Scotty Moore nor Bill Black attended Gladys's funeral.

1946 After the death of his mother, Elvis received over 35,000 messages of condolence.

1947 The Official Elvis Presley Fan Club of Great Britain and the Commonwealth sent a beautiful wreath for Gladys's funeral. It was shaped like a cross and made of red roses and carnations.

1948 Gladys Presley lived at Graceland for only a year and a half. After her death, Minnie Mae Presley ran the house.

1949 Shortly after his mother's death, Elvis wanted to quit show business. He stated that he wanted to go away and travel for awhile.

1950 After Gladys's death, Elvis carried one of her nightgowns as a security blanket.

1951 Based on the known history, the Smith family's life expectancy was approximately 38 years, while the Presley family's was 80-90 years.

1952 Prior to 1958, Joseph Esposito lived at 940 N. Trumbell Street in Chicago.

1953 Beginning in the late 1950's, Elvis rented out movie theaters in Memphis so he and his friends could enjoy a movie without the interference of his fans. The first theater he rented was the Avon in West Memphis.

1954 On being listed as a songwriter, Elvis had this to say in 1958: "It's all a big hoax. I never wrote a song in my life. I get a third of the credit for recording it. It makes me look smarter than I am. I've never even had an idea for a song — just once and maybe!"

John Smith, Elvis's uncle.

1955   Elvis was a member of the "Teen & Twenty Disc Club." His membership number was 11321.

1956   The Recording Industry Association of America (R.I.A.A.) was formed in 1958.

1957   None of Elvis's pre-1958 gold or platinum records were R.I.A.A. certified.

1958   Beginning in September of 1958, all Elvis records in Great Britain were sold under the RCA-Victor label. Prior to that time, they had been sold under RCA's HMV label.

1959   The first book written about Elvis by a foreign author was *The Sounding Story*, written in 1958 by Peter de Vecchi of Germany.

1960   Elvis visited his mother's grave at Forest Hill Cemetary on his motorcycle.

1961   A few months after Gladys's burial, a chip was found in the lower right hand corner of her gravestone.

1962   Gladys Presley's body was exhumed and placed in a mausoleum in Forest Hill Cemetery in order to prevent theft or damage to her grave. The mausoleum was located a few hundred yards from her original grave site.

1963   When Gladys Presley's casket was exhumed for placement in the mausoleum at Forest Hill Cemetery, it took 11 crew workers and four cemetery officials to do the job. Two newsmen were also on hand to record the transfer.

1964   The Presley room in the mausoleum at Forest Hill Cemetery was located to the right of the foyer. A bronze ornamental door opened onto the crypt.

1965 An anonymous person left a single red rose on Gladys's empty grave after her casket was exhumed and placed in the mausoleum.

1966 Citing back problems, Vernon Presley went into retirement in 1958 at the age of 42.

1967 Gladys's original gravestone was stored in the garage at Graceland after her body was moved from Forest Hill Cemetery to Graceland's Meditation Gardens.

1968 In October of 1958, RCA-Victor released the final Elvis Presley 78 rpm record, "One Night"/"I Got Stung" (20-7410). It was also released as a 45 rpm record (47-7410).

1969 On October 14, 1958, England's BBC-TV show *Six-Five Specia* featured Elvis singing "You're A Heartbreaker" while several impersonators lip-synched to the song.

1970 A 1958 *US TV* magazine poll of the most popular stars listed Elvis as #1 — by a ratio of 150 to 7!

1971 An RCA Red Seal label was used on Elvis' Golden Records album (RB-16069) in England.

1972 "All Shook Up" was a big hit in Russia in 1958/59.

1973 The Convair 880 airplane Elvis bought in the 1970's and renamed "Lisa Marie" was built in December of 1958 by General Dynamics in San Diego, California. It was first used by Delta Airlines as plane #912.

1974 In 1958, Elvis earned $2 million!

1975 The January 8, 1959, episode of *American Bandstand* was dedicated to Elvis in honor of his birthday.

1976 RCA-Victor released the album *For LP Fans Only* (LPM-1990) on February 9, 1959.

1977 In 1959, it was reported that Colonel Parker was going to write a book about Elvis's life and career, but he never did.

1978 Arthur Hooten became Elvis's personal aide at Graceland in 1959.

1979 In 1959, at a disc jockey convention at the American Hotel in Miami Beach, Florida, the Colonel gave out photo postcards of Elvis to everyone in the lobby.

1980 In April of 1959, RCA-Victor released the EP *A Touch of Gold, Vol. 1* (EPA-5088). The record came with a fan club membership card.

1981 Elvis's first credit card was American Express, which he obtained in the late 1950's. The card number was 115-002-750-6 and the expiration date was April 30, 1959. On the application, Elvis listed his home address as 661 Madison Avenue, Memphis.

1982 In the late spring of 1959, *TV Star Parade* magazine ran a contest called "My Experience with Elvis Presley." Contestants had to compose a story about an actual meeting with Elvis, about seeing his first movie, or about their feelings about any of his songs. First prize was $100; the contest deadline was August 5, 1959.

1983 In the late 1950's, Elvis received an average of 100 interview request phone calls a day.

1984 In the middle to late 1950's, Elvis's favorite hymn was "I Won't Have to Cross Jordan Alone."

1985 RCA-Victor released the 45 rpm record of "Big Hunk O' Love"/"My Wish Came True" (47-7600) in July of 1959.

1986 RCA-Victor released the *A Touch of Gold, Vol. 2* EP (EPA-5101) in September of 1959.

1987 On October 12, 1959, Colonel Parker wrote a $200 check to the Memphis Orchestral Society as a contribution to the drive to fund a symphony orchestra in Memphis.

1988 The October 12, 1959, issue of the Oxford University magazine *Isis* featured a front cover photo and a two-page article about Elvis.

1989 Elvis's cousin, Thomas Eugene Smith, was 25 years old when he was arrested and jailed for drunk driving. He lived at 1241 E. Mallory in Memphis. He sometimes toured with Elvis.

1990 In 1959, Elvis said that he did not like his teeth or his smile.

1991 Jessie D. Pressley, Vernon's father, filed a lawsuit against Legacy Records in the spring of 1959. He was suing for royalties for three TV appearances he had made—for a total of $298.93!

1992 In 1959, approximately 260 students from Kansas made the 720 mile trip to Memphis to obtain blades of grass from Graceland for their personal collections.

1993 In 1959, some critics named the three greatest threats to the world in the 1950's as the H-bomb, the winter flu, and Elvis Presley!

1994 The September 13, 1959, issue of *Melody Maker* magazine included an article by C. King entitled "Elvis: The Living Legend."

1995 In 1958/59, Elvis kept an 8x10 photo of his mother and father in his bedroom.

1996 Vernon had a special 1957 colorized promotional photo of Elvis tacked to the wall of his office in the late 1950's.

1997 On October 27, 1959, a 75 mph wind storm ripped through northern England. Meteorologists named the storm "Elvis."

1998 B.F. Wood Music Company held the British rights to Elvis's songs in the late 1950's.

1999 *TV Star Parade* held popularity polls for Elvis in 1959. In July, 30,218 were pro-Elvis and 932 were anti-Elvis. In June, 22,619 were pro-Elvis and 881 were anti-Elvis.

2000 In the November 1959 issue of *Teen* magazine, the "Cool Cat Comic" by Jack O'Brien featured the Cool Cat at a jukebox with a record flying out of it. A kitten, sitting on a couch, sips on a soda. The Cool Cat says, "That Elvis was really a 'way out' kitten!"

2001 In November of 1959, TV *Radio Mirror* magazine held a "Win a Present From a Star" contest. Prizes included an Elvis Presley portable Victrola with albums, Paul Anka's original manuscript of Lonely Boy, Frankie Avalon's bulky red sweater, Edd Byrnes's gold ID bracelet, Bobby Darin's record albums, Fabian's sport shirt, Connie Francis's transistor radio, Will Hutchins' cowboy boots, Johnny Mathis' record albums, Sal Mineo's bongo drums, Ricky Nelson's brownie starmatic camera, and John Smith's barbecue apron and spice set.

Elvis poses with several fans in California as they flash their beloved Fan Club packets filled with photos and other goodies.

Fan Club Facts

When Elvis Presley began his meteoric rise to fame in the 1950's, he very quickly gained the attention and love of millions of people. Fan clubs began to spring up across the nation. Following are a few facts regarding only a small portion of the hundreds of fan clubs devoted to the King of Rock 'n' Roll that sprang up across the nation during the early years.

1 *The Blue Moon Boys Fan Club*, headquartered at Sun Studios, was founded on September 9, 1954 by Marion Keisker. It might very well have been the first Elvis Presley fan club, although this club featured the entire Blue Moon Boys group.

2 *The Dallas Elvis Presley Fan Club* was said to have been the first Elvis fan club in Dallas, Texas. It was started in the fall of 1954, and was possibly the first Elvis Presley fan club in the state.

3 *The Elvis Presley Fan Club*, founded in June 1955 by Valerie Harms, has claimed to be the first Elvis fan club.

4 *The Elvis Presley Fan Club* located at 3929 Amherst, Dallas, Texas, was founded in late 1955 by Kate Wheeler after she found herself defending Elvis when her disc jockey friend insulted him. The club had over 20,000 members by February 1956.

5   In the 1950's, the *Los Angeles Elvis Presley Fan Club*'s president was Barbara Katsaros. Her sister, Almira, acted as vice-president.

6   In the 1950's, the *Elvis International Fan Club Worldwide*'s president was Georgianna King.

7   *The Official Elvis Presley Fan Club of Great Britain—Worldwide*, the first Elvis Presley fan club in Great Britain, opened in 1956. It was founded by Jeannie Seward, and was based out of Box 4, Leicester, England. Vice president of the club was Douglas Sartees.

8   The President of the *Elvis Presley National Fan Club*, P.O. Box 417, Madison, Tennessee, was Charlie Lamb.

9   *The Elvis' Angels Fan Club* was one of the first Elvis Presley fan clubs to open in Beverly Hills, California, in 1956.

10   *The Elvis Presley Fan Club* in O'Fallan, Missouri, was run by president Joyce Gentry. It was established in 1956.

11   In 1956, Jeanelle Alexander was President of the *Shreveport Bossier Elvis Presley Fan Club*.

12   *The Official Elvis Presley Fan Club* was opened by sugar heiress Judy Spreckles in Lancaster, California, in mid 1956.

13   *The King's Servants Fan Club* in Sara, Mississippi, was presided over by Joyce Sinquefield in the 1950's.

14   *The Elvis Presley Fan Club of the Hudson Valley* operated from 260 Elvis Presley Drive in Stone Ridge, New York.

15 *The Elvis Presley Suedettes Fan Club* opened in 1957. Its president was Charlotte Joseph. It was based at 155 N. 7th Street in Zanesville, Ohio.

16 *The Presley 'Crooner' Club* was opened in 1957 by Helen Shephard from Willisboro, North Carolina.

17 *The El-Kats Fan Club* was opened in 1957 by Mardele Ivan. Its address was 3763 Senasac Avenue, Long Beach 8, California.

18 *The Elvis Presley Fan Club of the Renton District* opened in 1957. President Pat Hindes ran the club from 11645 S.E. 102nd Street in Renton, Virginia.

19 *The Elvis Presley National Fan Club* received over five thousand letters a day in 1957. Their address was P.O. Box 94, Hollywood, California.

20 *The Elvis Presley Fan Club* at 9945 N.E. Sandy Street in Portland, Oregon opened in 1957 and was run by president Mitzi LaChapelle.

21 *The Elvis Presley Fan Club* located at 92 Madison Avenue in Bergenfield, New Jersey, was run by Mary Lou Colontrelle in 1957.

22 *The Elvis Presley Fan Club* in Chicago, Illinois was formed in 1957. The president was Arlene Cogin and the headquarters were located at 6049 N. Central Park.

23 *The Elvis Presley Kats Fan Club* was started in 1957 by Holly Smith, Jr. It was located on Middle Run Road in Chester, West Virginia.

24 *The I Hate Elvis Presley Fan Club* was formed in Ann Arbor, Michigan, in 1957. It offered membership cards with razor blades attached to them; the cards read, "He makes me feel surgical—like cutting my throat."

25   *The Elvis Presley Fan Club* at 91 Maxwell Avenue in Geneva, New York, opened in 1957. Its president was Martha Currie.

26   *The Push for Presley Fan Club* at 3530 Yorbalinda in Royal Oaks, Michigan, was founded in 1957 by Maureen Minnelso.

27   *The Elvis Presley Fan Club* at 323 Isabella Avenue in Irvington, New Jersey, was founded by Diane Kress in 1957.

28   *The Elvis Presley Teenage Fan Club* was founded in 1957.

29   *The Elvis Presley Fan Club of Twin Hills* in Dallas, Texas, was founded in 1957 and run by Judy Thorp.

30   *The Elvis Presley Adult-Over 21 Fan Club* was established in 1957 by C. Hank. It was based in Staunton, Illinois.

31   *The Presley Kittens Fan Club* was started in 1957. Linda Leistritz was the president and the club was located at 4621 Dahlia, St. Louis 16, Missouri.

32   *The Sideburn Set Fan Club* was opened in 1957 by Judy Barkan. The address of the club was 120 Upland Drive, San Francisco, California.

33   *The Elvis Presley Fan Club* based at 858 West Chalmers Place in Chicago, Illinois, was opened by Sophie Haroutunian.

34   *The Elvis Presley Fan Club* located at 749 N. Myers Street in Burbank, California, was run by president Nancie Anderson in 1957.

35   *The Elvis Presley Fan Club* in Ontario, Canada, was opened in 1957 by Elaine Little. It was based at 61 Collinson Blvd. in Downsview.

36   *The Elvis Presley Fan Club* at 465 N. Spalding Avenue in Lebanon, Kentucky, was run by Anne Laurel Parrott. It was opened in 1957.

37   *The Elvis Presley Fan Club of Buffalo, NY* opened in 1957. The president was Robert J. Banks and his address was 51 Forman Place, Buffalo, 11, New York.

38   In 1957, the *Elvis Presley Fan Club* located at 205 155th Place in Calumet City, Illinois, was run by Pat Chumley.

39   *The Living End Elvis Presley Fan Club* located at 6108 N. Nassau in Chicago, Illinois, was founded by Sue Dessimoz in 1957.

40   *The All Valley Elvis Presley Fan Club* was founded by Mary Jean Bland in 1957. Its address was P.O. Box 324, Edinburg, Texas.

41   In 1957, *The Elvis Presley Fan Club* run by Linda Deutsch was located at 510 Brinley Avenue in Bradley Beach, New Jersey.

42   In 1957, the *Elvis Really Has It All Fan Club* located at 220 75th Street in Bayside, New York, was run by Roslyn Dishotsky.

43   *The Prez Cuts Fan Club* could be reached at Box 251, Ocean City, Maryland. It was founded in 1957, and Johnny Purcell served as club president.

44   *The Elvis Presley Fan Club* of Long Beach, CA was opened in 1957 by Barbie Herald.

45   *The Presley-ette Fan Club* was opened by Beverly Rook. Its address was 1510 W. Wardlow Road, Long Beach, 10, California.

46 *The Elvis Presley Fan Club of British Columbia* in Canada was run by Joyce Dodds. Its address was 1026 W. 13th Avenue.

47 *The Robinson Intermediate Fan Club*, founded in 1956, was located in Wichita, Kansas.

48 *Another Elvis Presley Fan Club* was started in 1957 by Barbara Barnes Sims, who worked for Sun Studios from 1957 to 1960. She answered all of Elvis's fan mail.

49 *The Elvis Presley Fan Club of Japan* was run by Hideo Okamura of Tokyo.

50 *The Elvis Presley Fan Club of Dayton, OH* opened in 1958. Eloise Peggs was the president.

51 Roberta Renee was the president of *The Elvis Presley Fan Club of San Diego, CA*.

52 By 1959, the *E.P. Continentals Fan Club* was reportedly the largest Elvis Presley fan club, boasting over 20,000 members.

1935 Facts

1 In 1935, the year Elvis was born, the United States was still in the throes of the Great Depression, with unemployment at a staggering 17% nationwide.

2 The President of the United States in 1935 was Franklin Delano Roosevelt and the Vice-President was John Nance Garner.

3 A loaf of bread cost 8¢ and a gallon of milk cost 46¢ in 1935.

4 In 1935, the development of an "artificial heart" and of a man-made "bloodstream" by Col. Charles A. Lindbergh and Professor Alexis Carrel was announced by the Rockefeller Institute for Medical Research. Their work enabled science to keep organs alive outside the body,

5 Sir Robert Watson-Watt patented "radar" on April 2, 1935. Nylon was also patented in 1935, and the Richter scale for measuring the intensity of earthquakes was developed.

6 The infamous "Lindbergh Baby" trial of Bruno R. Hauptmann began on January 2, 1935 in Flemington, New Jersey. The trial lasted until February 13, at which time Hauptmann was convicted of the first degree murder of Charles A. Lindbergh, Jr.

7 James J. Braddock beat Max Baer in a 15-round decision to become the heavyweight boxing champion of the world on June 13, 1935.

8   The first wearable hearing aides were introduced in 1935.

9   The top movies in 1935 were *Mutiny On the Bounty*, *The Informer*, *G-Men*, *Captain Blood*, *A Midsummer Night's Dream*, *The Littlest Rebel*, and *The Bride of Frankenstein*.

10 *Mutiny on the Bounty*, produced by Irving Thalberg and Albert Lewis, won the "Best Picture" Oscar for the year 1935.

11 *Little Lulu* debuted in comic books in 1935.

12 "Krueger Cream Ale" was sold by the Krueger Brewing Company based in Richmond, Virginia. This was the first appearance of beer in a can.

13 *Your Hit Parade* and *Fibber McGee & Molly* debuted on the radio in 1935.

14 Alcoholics Anonymous was formed by Dr. Robert Smith and William Wilson in 1935.

15 The 1935 World Series saw the Detroit Tigers beat the Chicago Cubs 4 games to 2. It was the 32nd World Series.

16 Home run king Babe Ruth was released by the New York Yankees and went on to play for the Boston Braves. He hit his 714th and final home run on May 25 , 1935, against the Pirates.

17 A gallon of gas cost 19¢ in 1935.

18 The lie detector was used for the very first time in a courtroom in Portage, Wisconsin, in 1935.

19 In 1935, the first automatic parking meter was installed.

20 Sammy Snead, twenty-two, became the youngest professional golfer in 1935.

21 In 1935, Benny Goodman was the "King of Swing," and rising band leaders included Tommy Dorsey and Glenn Miller.

22 The top songs in 1935 were "Cheek to Cheek," "Summertime," "I Got Plenty of Nothin'," "Just One of Those Things," "Red Sails in the Sunset," "Lovely to Look At," "Maybe," "Lullaby of Broadway," "Stairway to the Stars," and "When I Grow Too Old to Dream."

23 The average cost of a three bedroom home in 1935 was $3,400.

24 The Social Security Act became law on August 14, 1935.

25 The WPA (Works Progress Administration) was enacted, putting thousands to work building bridges and roads, including Vernon Presley!

26 The average cost of a new car in 1935 was $540.

27 The 1935 Orange Bowl, the first ever, featured Bucknall vs. Miami.

28 The 1935 Sugar Bowl, the first ever, featured Tulane vs. Temple.

29 The average family income in 1935 was $1,784.

30 Will Rogers and Wiley Post were killed in an Alaskan plane crash on August 15, 1935.

31 Controversial Louisiana politician Huey Long was assassinated at the Baton Rouge Capitol building on September 8, 1935.

32 Fashion designer Nolan Miller was born on the same day as Elvis: January 8, 1935.

33 Other famous people born in 1935 include Floyd Patterson, Bob Denver, "The Amazing Kreskin," Tippi Hedren, A.J. Foyt, and Sam Cooke.

34 Actress Mary Pickford divorced Douglas Fairbanks, Jr., and Ozzie Nelson married Harriet Hilliard in 1935.

35 The new Parker Brothers board game, Monopoly, went on sale for the first time on December 31, 1935.

Tupelo Facts

1. When the area of the Mississippi River now known as Tupelo was discovered by explorers in the 1500's, it was inhabited by the Chickasaw Indians.

2. In the late 1600's, Jacques Marquette, a Jewish missionary, and Louis Joliet voyaged down the Mississippi, creating the first accurate record of the river's course. Their travels led them through what is now Tupelo.

3. In 1650, the Monsoupelas Indians raided the Mississippi Valley and fought with the French against the Chickasaw Indians. The Monsoupeleas were defeated by the cunning and stronger Chickasaws.

4. The Ackia Battlefield, located outside Tupelo, was the site of a battle between the the Chickasaw Indians, who were armed with British artillery, and the combined forces of the French and the Chocktaw Indians. The battle, which began on May 26, 1736, was over the Ackia, Apeony, and Chikafalaya villages.

5. By 1832, the Chickasaw Indians had been forced off their land in Tupelo.

6. The Battle of Tupelo began on July 14, 1864, after Confederate Lt. General Nathan Bedford Forrest gave orders to stop the railroad which transported supplies for the Union Army. General William Tecumseh Sherman led the Union Army which tried to protect the railroad.

7   Lee County, Mississippi, was established on December 10, 1866. It was named after the famous general Robert E. Lee.

8   Lee County was formed from parts of Itawamba County in the east and Pontontoc County in the west.

9   Lee County is surrounded by Prentiss, Union, Itawamba, Monroe, Pontontoc, and Chickasaw counties.

10   Lee County measures 418 square miles.

11   Our research shows that, on April 15, 1867, the first officers elected in Lee County were probate judge Jacob Bardin, probate clerk D.P. Cypert, circuit clerk A.J. Cockran, sheriff J.M. Dillard, assessor A.M. Robinson, county supervisor W.A. Dozier, coroner Robert Gray, rnager W.R. Hampton, and county attorney J.L. Finley.

12   According to our research, Lee County school commissioners in 1867 were G.C. Thomason, E.G. Thomas, John B. Sparks, and Rev. J.D. Russell.

13   Colonel J.D. Wilson and Hugh H. Martin were the first representatives of Lee County in the Lower House, according to our research.

14   Our research shows that the first state senator for Mississippi was Colonel John M. Simonton.

15   The city of Tupelo was found by British settlers on July 20, 1872.

16   The city of Tupelo became incorporated in the 1870's.

17   Tupelo was built on Chickasaw Indian land.

18   The name Tupelo comes from the Chickasaw word *topala*, which which means "lodging place."

19   The word Tupelo is also an Indian word for a gum tree.

20   The main livelihood of Tupelo and the surrounding regions was based on cotton and raising cattle.

21   The Tombigbee River is the body of water nearest Tupelo.

22   The Natchez Trace, measuring 400 miles in length, connects Natchez, Mississippi, and Nashville, Tennessee. Created over 8000 years ago by Indians as a route of commerce, it was also used by boatmen, the military, and the mail service. The Trace passes through several towns and cities, including Tupelo, Jackson, and Kosuisko.

23   In 1887, railroads erected in the Tupelo area included the Mobile-Ohio line and the Kansas City-Memphis-Birmingham line.

24   In 1901, Tupelo was chosen as the site of the first U.S. Fish Hatchery.

25   In 1914, Lee County became the location of a 49 mile stretch of hard-surfaced highway, the first concrete road in the state of Mississippi.

26   John Rankin served as the congressman of Tupelo from 1920 to 1952.

27   The location of the Battle of Tupelo was established as a National Battlefield by the city of Tupelo on February 21, 1929.

28   In 1933, Tupelo became the first U.S. city to purchase and use electrical power from the Tennessee Valley Authority.

29 At two different times, Tupelo was named the "All American City."

30 On Sunday, April 5, 1936 at 9 p.m., Tupelo was hit by a devestating tornado. Approximately 235 people were killed and an additional 1100 were injuredc. Although 48 city blocks were destroyed, the Presley home was spared.

31 After the April 5th tornado, the historic Lyric Theater was used as a morgue where families came to identify the bodies of their loved ones. People who lost their homes in the storm used railroad box cars for shelter.

32 By the fall of 1936, the town of Tupelo was wired for electricity as part of the REA electrification program. Unfortunately, the Presleys were unable to afford such a luxury at the time.

33 In 1940, the population of Tupelo numbered 5800.

Memphis Facts

1. On May 14, 1795, Don Manuel Gayoso de Lemos, governor of Louisiana in the 1780's, bought a large section of the lower bluffs of the Mississippi Valley for the sum $30,000. It is today known as the city of Memphis.

2. In 1811 and 1812, the mid-south, including Memphis and Tupelo, was ravaged by deadly earthquakes.

3. In October of 1818, the Chickasaw Indians ceded 5000 acres of their land to the United States. The treaty they signed was negotiated by Issac Shelby.

4. Memphis was founded by James Winchester, John Overton, and Andrew Jackson on May 22, 1819.

5. In 1819, James Winchester named the city of Memphis after an Egyptian city. Translated, the word means, "good abode."

6. The city of Memphis was incorporated in 1826.

7. The *Memphis Appeal* newspaper was started in 1840.

8. Memphis and South Memphis merged in 1850.

9. By the mid-1850's, Memphis had grown to be the 6th largest city in the nation.

10 In 1857, the Memphis and Charleston railroad was completed, linking the Atlantic Ocean and the Mississippi River.

11 On June 6, 1862, a Union Army fleet defeated a Confederate naval force in the Battle of Memphis.

12 In June of 1862, General Ulysses S. Grant planned the historical Vicksburg campaign at the Hunt-Phelan home in Memphis. He used this building as his headquarters during the Civil War.

13 From 1877 to 1879, over 5,000 people died as a result of a yellow fever epidemic in Memphis. An additional 25,000 people fled the city.

14 As a result of the yellow fever epidemic, the city of Memphis went bankrupt and lost its charter in 1879

15 In 1887, artesian well water becomes available in Memphis for the first time.

16 The Orpheum Theater opened in 1890, replacing the famous Grand Opera House.

17 In 1893, Memphis regained its charter and rebuilding of the city was in full swing.

18 The first public library in Memphis, Cossitt Library, opened in 1893.

19 The first skyscraper in Memphis, the ten-story Porter Building, opens in 1895.

20 Robert Church, a freed slave, became the first African-American millionare in the South in 1899. A resident of Memphis, he made his

fortune in real estate and other business ventures.

21 Church's Park and Auditorium, the first entertainment center for African-Americans in Memphis, opened in 1899.

22 W.C. Handy wrote the first blues song on BealeStreet in 1909.

23 Clarence Saunders opens the first Piggly Wiggly supermarket in Memphis in 1916.

24 The city of Memphis measures 295.5 square miles.

25 The county of Shelby, of which Memphis is a part, measures 772 square miles.

26 On several occasions in the 1950's, Memphis was named the quietest, cleanest, and safest city in the U.S.

27 Kemmons Wilson opened the first Holiday Inn hotel, located on Summer Avenue in Memphis, in 1952.

Coming Soon!

Elvis, The Movie Years
A 2001 Fact Odyssey

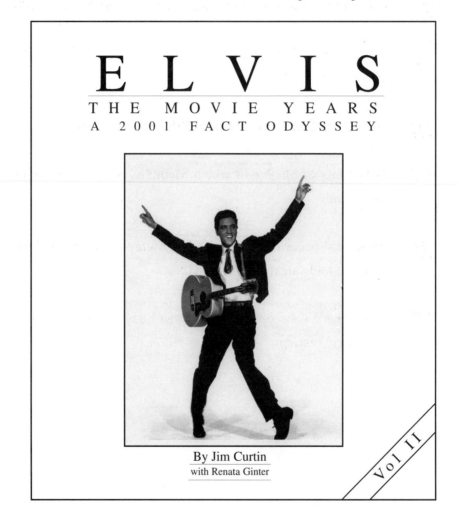

Elvis expert Jim Curtin reveals 2001 facts about Elvis's films.